M4 SHERMAN

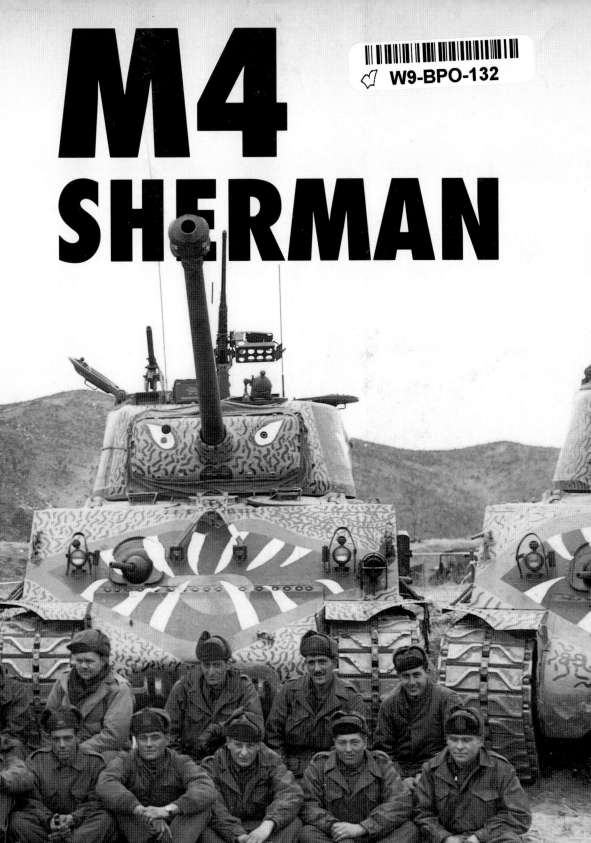

Michael Green

Motorbooks International
Publishers & Wholesalers ®

*To my good friend
Jacques M. Littlefield whose help and
support has allowed me to complete
this book and many others.*

First published in 1993 by Motorbooks
International Publishers & Wholesalers, PO
Box 2, 729 Prospect Avenue, Osceola, WI
54020 USA

© Michael Green, 1993

Motorbooks International is a certified
trademark, registered with the United States
Patent Office

The information in this book is true and
complete to the best of our knowledge. All
recommendations are made without any
guarantee on the part of the author or
Publisher, who also disclaim any liability
incurred in connection with the use of this
data or specific details

We recognize that some words, model names
and designations, for example, mentioned
herein are the property of the trademark
holder. We use them for identification
purposes only. This is not an official
publication

Motorbooks International books are also
available at discounts in bulk quantity for
industrial or sales-promotional use. For details
write to Special Sales Manager at the
Publisher's address

Library of Congress Cataloging-in-Publication
Data

  Green Michael.
    M4 Sherman tank/Michael Green.
      p. cm.
  Includes index.
  ISBN 0-87938-803-X
  1. Sherman tank. I. Title.
  UG446.5.G693   1993
  358'.1883– –dc20   93-7459

Printed in Hong Kong

On the front cover: An M4 Sherman tank in
Korea shortly after the end of the Korean War.
Ed Phelps, Jr.

On the back cover: Top, a 76mm Sherman
with US Army paratroopers sometime in the
early 1950s. Lower right, an M4A3 Sherman in
the mountains of Italy during World War II.
Lower left, a Duplex Drive Sherman tank has
its large canvas waterproof flotation screen
half-collapsed. As all the air within the screen
is let out, the entire assembly will be folded
into place around the bottom hull of the
vehicle and held in place by elastic bands
attached to metal rings. *US Army*

On the title page: Men of the 89th Tank
Battalion, 25th Infantry Division, US Army,
pose in front of their animal face painted
M4A3 Sherman tanks on March 1, 1951. The
painting of American tanks with fierce animal
faces and the effect it had on Chinese soldiers
is unknown. But it did allow a measure of
individual expression not always found in
military service and no doubt improved
morale. *US Army*

On the frontispiece: A war-weary M4 patrols
a narrow country road. *US Army*

Acknowledgments

Special thanks for help in putting this
book together go to Dick Hunnicutt,
Dennis Riva, Richard Bryd, Fred Ropkey,
Skip Warvel, Fred Pernell, Donald L.
Gilleland, Dennis R. Spence, William F.
Atwater, Kenneth Powers, Jim Mesko,
Samuel Katz, Michael O'Brien, William
U. Rosenmund, Chris Foss, Major J. Russell (Canadian Army), George Bradford,
Dr. Robert Wright, Steven Zaloga,
Clarence Lancy, Roy Hamilton, Bill Nahmens, David Fetcher, and George Forty.

Organizations that kindly extended
their help were the 5th Armored Division
Association, *AFV News*, *Armor* Magazine, The Patton Museum, The Ordnance
Museum at Aberdeen Proving Ground,
Maryland, *Marine Corps Gazette*, U. S.
Army Center for Military History, the National Archives, and the British Army
Tank Museum.

The author would like to extend a
special note of appreciation for Colonels
William A. Hamberg, Erling J. Foss, James
H. Leach, and Henry A. Gardiner for
sharing their stories and answering many
questions as this book was completed.

Contents

Introduction

The Sherman has to be the best known American tank ever built. Through the years, the Sherman has symbolized the US Army in World War II. With almost 50,000 produced between 1942 and 1945, the Sherman tank served in almost every part of the globe during the war. Not only did this mass-produced vehicle equip the armored formations of the US Army and Marine Corps, but it also saw service with a whole host of allied armies including the Free French, Russian, Indian, Canadian, New Zealand, Polish, and British.

The name Sherman was borrowed from the British. During the war, the British Army nicknamed all American-built tanks in its inventory after Civil War generals. Hence, the M3 medium tank supplied to the British in the early days of the war was named the General Grant. When the British received the M4 series of tanks, they nicknamed it the General Sherman. Most soldiers dropped the General part and decided to call the tank the Sherman or the M4 (no matter what model of the M4 series they were using).

During the war, the Sherman proved to be a study in contrast. The American public saw this tank as an invincible land battleship dashing around battlefields blowing up or running over anything that stood in its path. American wartime pro-paganda created this image on purpose; Hollywood later perpetuated the idea through its war movies. So strong is this image that even today many people perceive the word tank and the word Sherman as being one in the same.

For many American and Allied tankers who used the Sherman in combat the view from inside the tank looking out was not a pretty one. Underarmored and undergunned when compared to most late-war German tanks, the Sherman was also easy prey to a wide variety of German antitank weapons ranging from hand-held rocket launchers to towed anti-tank guns like the famous 88.

The Sherman has not always been considered underprotected. When the tank first saw combat in 1942 with the British Army in North Africa, it was considered almost on par with the leading edge of tank technology. Yet, when the invasion of Europe began in June 1944, the Sherman turned out to be almost obsolete when fighting German tanks.

The reason for this sudden inequality had numerous roots. The most important was US military doctrine, which stressed the Sherman's role as a mass-produced exploitation vehicle and not as a vehicle designed to engage in combat with enemy tanks. This job was to be left to specialized tank destroyers. Combat experi-ence in the war later proved this doctrine to be seriously flawed. By the time American military leaders realized this fact, it was too late to produce new tanks or to upgrade the Sherman enough to be more on par with German tanks.

During the war, the Germans and Russians engaged in a tank technology race. Americans, who lacked experience in large-scale tank warfare between 1942 and mid-1944, were seriously handi-capped. While the German and Russian armies were engaging in massive tank battles involving thousands of tanks on either side, the US Army in North Africa and later in Italy never saw more than a few dozen enemy tanks at any one time.

Back in the United States, the at-tempts at keeping the M4 a viable com-bat vehicle were hampered by too many people being involved in the process. Different Army departments interpreted differently the results of combat experi-ence and intelligence data on enemy weapon systems. During the war, three main players were to work together to de-sign and develop the M4. The Army Ground Forces (AGF) was to decide what type of tank the army needed. The Ar-mored Board was to do the tactical test-ing on the tanks the AGF requested. Last but not least, the Ordnance Branch was to do the engineering testing of prototype

An M36 Tank Destroyer armed with a 90mm gun passes a destroyed German Mark IV medium tank near Langlir, Belgium, on January 13, 1945. The M36's 90mm gun was the only American gun to take on and destroy the German Panther and Tiger tanks. *US Army*

tanks the AGF requested and ordered from civilian contractors.

In reality during the war, the AGF could never figure out what they wanted in a tank. So it was left to the Ordnance Branch and its officers to come up with tank and weapon concepts. While many of its ideas proved to be most promising, much of what Ordnance attempted during the war was done based on seat-of-the-pants deductions and gut feelings instead of scientific analysis and combat-units input. This method of tank development led to constant quarrels that effectively delayed the fielding of an M4 replacement until the war ended.

What success the US Army achieved with the M4 tank during World War II was due more to American and Allied superiority in the air and in artillery support than any distinguishing element of the tank's design. In the end, the quantity of M4s overwhelmed the German war machine.

Not until the mid-1950s, when the Israeli Defense Forces began to upgrade its imported M4 tanks with improved guns and engines, did people realize the soundness and great flexibility of the vehicle's design. In the numerous wars in which Israel fought against its Arab neighbors, the Shermans, upgraded by Israel, constantly bested newer post-war tanks that the Soviet Union supplied to its Arab allies.

This book is not the complete combat history of the Sherman tank. Considering the scope of the Sherman's use since 1942, a complete history would require a multi-volume series beyond the goals of this author and publisher. Instead, the author presents an overview of the Sherman, its development, and some examples of its combat career. Most important, it may provide for the reader a feeling of what it would be like to be inside the Sherman tank looking out!

Chapter 1

Design of the M4 Sherman

The German Mark IV medium tank had a dramatic effect on future American tank design. Prior to the German attacks on Poland and France, the US Army had spent most of its time and limited funds developing light tanks armed mainly with machine guns.

This is not to say that the US Army completely neglected developing medium tanks. In late 1936, the Army recommended developing the T5 medium tank. The T5 was essentially an enlarged version of the Army's M3 light tank. Using many of the M3's components, the T5 was supposed to have more firepower and armor protection than other American tanks then in service. Starting in early 1939, a number of T5 prototype tanks were tested with a combination of different cannons and machine guns. The T5

was standardized in late 1939 as the M2 and M2A1 medium tanks and armed with a 37mm cannon and six machine guns. This vehicle proved to be the forerunner of the Sherman, although the Sherman wouldn't reach production for another three years.

On August 15, 1940, the US Army entered into a contract with Chrysler Corp. for the production of 1,000 M2A1s at the rate of 100 a month. But because reports from Europe indicated that the M2A1 would be obsolete before it was built, the Army abruptly canceled the

contract on August 28. Instead, Chrysler was asked to build 1,000 new, as yet undesigned, M3 medium tanks. The M3s would have thicker armor than the M2A1 and would be armed with a 75mm gun, like the German Army Mark IV medium tank.

The M3 Tank

The machines and skills needed to build a large turret mounting a 75mm gun didn't exist in the United States and would take time to develop. The Army, therefore, decided to adopt a tank design with a hull-mounted 75mm gun. The Army had already developed an experimental design based on the T5, which mounted a 75mm howitzer. Known as the T5E2, this vehicle featured the 75mm howitzer in the right front of the vehicle's hull. Tests had shown that this setup was practical for tank installation. (Minor

The M3 medium tank (based on the chassis of the M2 medium) had a hull-mounted 75mm gun as its main armament. Also mounted was a smaller turret on top of the vehicle's superstructure that was fitted with a 37mm gun and a single .30cal machine gun. By the time production stopped on the M3 series and its variants, almost 6,258 had been built. *US Army*

Shown during the invasion of Poland in 1939, the German Army Mark IV medium tank was armed with a short-barreled 75mm gun in a fully traversable turret. The Mark IV made a powerful impression on the US Army. In response to this German tank, the US Army began to develop the Sherman tank. *Armor Magazine collection*

ORDNANCE DEPARTMENT. A.P.G.
38653 – 8/23/39.   O.P.5402.
Medium Tank M2 Prodcution
Model No. 2. Three quarter
right front.

Looking much like the prototype T5 medium tank, the vehicle pictured is the M2 medium tank. Armed with a 37mm gun in its turret, the M2 also mounted as many as six .30cal machine guns, four of which were fired from the hull compartment. Basically a scaled-up M3 light tank, the M2 medium tank served as the basis for the later M4 Sherman tank series. *US Army*

modifications in test or production tanks were indicated by adding an E suffix to the vehicle test or model number.)

The Army told Chrysler that blueprints for the M3 would not be ready until November 1940. Chrysler engineers would not know until then what kind of and how many machine tools they would need to build this new tank. They decided, however, that the building to house the future tank factory could be erected

anyway. The Army and Chrysler picked a location for the factory that was 17mi from downtown Detroit and ground was broken on September 9, 1940. Located on 113 acres of farmland, the big question was how big the factory should be. Tanks had never been built in the United States on a production basis. No past performance charts existed. If the new tank factory was too small, Chrysler would be unable to meet production goals. If it was too large, Chrysler would look foolish.

The M3 was fitted with a 75mm cannon in a limited-traverse mount on the right side of the front hull sponson. A 37mm cannon was carried in a turret on top of the superstructure. The superstructure was built out of a combination of cast and welded steel plates riveted together. Later variants of the M3 featured numerous production differences, including a cast hull.

The M3 weighed about 30 tons and had a crew of six: the commander, a driver, two loaders, and two gunners. For secondary armament, the M3 had four machine guns fitted: two in the hull firing forward and two in the 37mm cannon armed turret. One was mounted alongside the 37mm cannon, the other on a large cupola on top of the vehicle. The M3's overall height was 10ft 3in.

The first production M3 tanks were powered by the 9cyl Curtiss-Wright radial air-cooled gasoline aircraft engine. Later models were fitted with either General Motors (GM) diesel water-cooled engines or 30cyl Chrysler multibank gasoline engines.

The final design work on the M3 tank was finished in February 1941. By August 1941, full-scale production had begun. The M3 was built until August 1942 with a total of 4,924 built.

The British Army, which lost the bulk of its tanks during the evacuation at Dunkirk (France), was a big user of the M3 tank. Since British industry did not have the ability to mass produce new tanks to replace their losses, the British bought over 1,000 M3s with a different 37mm gun turret. The British designation for their version of the M3 was the General Grant. Americans referred to their M3s as the General Lee. The British M3s first saw action in North Africa on May 27, 1942, when the Germans launched an attack on British forces stationed near the small desert town of Bir Hacheim. The 75mm cannon on the Grant tanks outranged both the German Mark III tank fitted with a 50mm cannon and the larger Mark IV tank fitted with a short-barreled 75mm cannon.

US Army units first saw action with M3s on November 28, 1942, when US and British forces took control of a small town in Tunisia, North Africa, and a near-by airfield from German forces. During the attack, American M3s suffered serious losses from hidden German antitank guns. Over the next few days, the inexperienced US tankers suffered additional heavy losses at the hands of the more experienced Germans.

Shortly after these battles and subsequent actions during the fighting at Kasserine Pass, the newly arrived M4s replaced the M3s. Some M3s served the remainder of the war fighting the Japanese in the Pacific and Far East. With little to fear from obsolete Japanese tanks, the M3 served with the British, US, and Australian units. About 1,300 M3 tanks were shipped to the Soviet Union under the Lend-Lease program.

The M3 tank had a number of serious shortcomings. The limited traverse of the hull-mounted 75mm gun meant the entire tank had to be turned if an enemy vehicle appeared almost anywhere but right in front of the main gun. The 75mm gun also had a low muzzle velocity, which meant its shells couldn't always penetrate the armor of enemy tanks. The M3's armor was also inadequate, so the US Army was anxious to field the Sherman medium tank, which was designed to correct these deficiencies. The US Army's main concern, however, was ease and speed of production and not building the world's best tank. As a result, the Sherman was orginally based on as many M3 medium tank components as possible. It was

hoped that this process would speed the Sherman's introduction into combat.

Beginnings of the Sherman

The following text is from a US Army Ordnance Report describing the changes involved in developing the M4 medium tank from the M3.

"The Ordnance Committee, in recommending military characteristics for Medium Tank M3 on 29 August 1940, directed that work on an improved tank with the 75-mm gun in the turret should start as soon as possible.

"Detailed characteristics for the improved tank were submitted by the Armored Force Board under date of 31 August 1940. In February 1941 the Chief of Ordnance requested the Aberdeen Proving Ground to proceed with the design of the new tank following completion of design work on Medium Tank M3.

"The Chief of Ordnance directed that automotive features of the new design, including power plant, power train, suspension, and track, should be essentially those of the M3. The principal change was to be the removal of the 75-mm gun from the right sponson to the turret and the elimination of the 37-mm gun. Some reduction in height of silhouette was suggested, as well as provision of anti-aircraft protection.

"At a conference at Aberdeen Proving Ground on 18 April 1941, five different designs were considered. It was

In August 1941, a full-size wooden mockup of a new vehicle designated the T6 medium tank is shown at Aberdeen Proving Ground, Maryland. Eventually, after a number of minor changes, the T6 became the M4 series of Sherman tanks when placed into production. *US Army*

agreed to retain the chassis of the Medium Tank M3, including the power plant and power train; that the top hull should use welded or cast armor; and that as many parts and components of the M3 as practicable should be used, in order to go into production at the earliest possible date. Major Armament would be mounted in a power-operated turret having 360-degree traverse, and an attempt would be made to increase the thickness of armor, reducing the size of the crew compartment and the number of crew members in order to achieve this without increasing the gross weight.

"It was agreed that a design embodying a cast turret large enough to accommodate the 75-mm gun M2, but otherwise similar to the turret of Medium Tank M3, should be used. The removable front plate of the turret, constituting the gun mount, was to be designed to accommodate any one of the following combinations:

"a. One 75-mm gun with one cal. .30 machine gun.

An early M4A1 medium tank undergoing
tests at Fort Knox, Kentucky, in the spring of
1942. The twin, fixed .30cal machine guns
mounted in the front hull was one feature of
these early production vehicles. Another
feature found only on very early vehicles is
the 75mm gun sight rotor located on top of
the turret. *US Army*

"b. Two 37-mm Guns M6 with one cal. .30 machine gun.

"c. One 105-mm howitzer with one cal. .30 machine gun.

"d. Three cal. .50 machine guns especially arranged for high-angle antiaircraft fire.

"e. One 6-pounder, high-velocity gun with one cal. .30 machine gun

"The advantages of this arrangement and choice of armament lay in the fact that, from a production standpoint, the most available weapons could be mounted; and, from a tactical standpoint, a standard tank could be fitted with varying armament to suit different missions.

"It was further agreed that a cal. .30 machine gun for antiaircraft fire should be mounted in the commander's cupola and that the two fixed cal. .30 machine guns in the bow for operation by the driver should be retained.

"Ordnance Committee action in May 1941 recommended building a full-size wooden model and a pilot model of the new tank, and designating it Medium Tank T6.

"The design was predicated upon the use of the Wright R-975-EC2 engine, but space was provided for installation of a Wright G-100 or G-200 engine, when available.

"Formal approval of these recommendations was recorded in June 1941.

"Upon completion of the wooden mock-up, Aberdeen Proving Ground was directed to assemble a tank with a cast hull, and Rock Island Arsenal to assemble a tank with a welded hull but without a turret. The design was corrected to reduce the number of plates required and the amount of welding.

"Aberdeen completed its pilot of the T6 on 2 September 1941, and after representatives of the Armored Force and the Ordnance Department had inspected the new tank at the Proving Ground, it was agreed to substitute an escape door in the floor for the side doors of the hull and to omit the cupola. A cal. .30 machine gun for antiaircraft use was to be mounted in the place formerly occupied by the cupola, if feasible.

"With these changes the tank was believed ready to go into production, and the Ordnance Committee recommended that the vehicle be standardized as Medium Tank M4. These recommendations were formally approved in October 1941. The characteristics were amended to provide for a cal. .50 antiaircraft machine gun, if practicable, and to provide for use of a ball mount for the bow gun.

"Placing the 75-mm gun in the turret permitted a 360deg traverse instead of the 15deg left and 15deg right of Medium Tank M3; elevation was from -12deg to 25deg instead of from -9deg to 20deg as in the M3. In the turret, the gunner had a better position, both for sighting and for comfort.

"The 75-mm gun breech was turned 90deg from the vertical, allowing for easy right-hand loading from the left-hand side and decreasing the overhead room required. The 75-mm gun was connected by an adjustable arm to a periscope sight rotor.

"By modification of design and an increase in the turret ring diameter from the 54 1/2in of the M3 tank to 69in, a larger turret basket was provided. The basket covering on the pilot model was of expanded metal screening. It was proposed to use perforated metal with 1/2in holes in the production models because this was lighter and could be procured more readily. Both of these screens were very light and they provided easy visual and sound communication between the basket and the fighting compartment, and good ventilation.

"The driver's seat was moved from above the transmission, as in the M3, to the left of the transmission, and an assistant driver's seat was provided at the right of the transmission. A transmission oil cooler was installed, which helped lower the ambient temperature in the fighting compartment. Width of the transmission oil pump gears was increased from 1/2in to 7/8in to increase the circulation of oil through the cooler. Three oil breathers were located on the final drive and one on the transmission to prevent pumping and overheating the oil. These changes also helped make the driver's position more comfortable.

"A driver's hatch was added for easy access to the driver's seat, and it was provided with a periscope for indirect vision. The driver's seat was made adjustable to permit the driver to sit with his head and shoulders above the hatch opening in noncombat areas. A direct-vision slot was also provided for the driver. Space was provided for transmitter and receiver radios.

"The mechanical 'long-lever' steering control was used instead of the Hycon booster type of steering. This simplification did away with a pump, sump tank, pressure reservoir, valves, and hydraulic piping.

"The instrument panel retained all of the previous instruments except that the magnetic starting switch was changed, together with a fuel gage and a transmission oil temperature indicator. Circuit breakers were substituted for the former fuses. Wiring was made more accessible.

"An inside pull control for the fire extinguishers was provided near the driver's seat, permitting instant action in case of a fire in the engine compartment.

"Elimination of the side doors made for a much safer hull and did away with some parts. An escape door was placed in the floor of the lower hull behind the assistant driver's seat.

"Omission of the cupola reduced the overall height 12in. Substitution of an antiaircraft gun on top of the turret and provision for two 360deg periscopes were expected to constitute great improvements.

"Four lifting eyes were welded to the upper hull to facilitate handling the tank for transportation. Shielding, integral with the upper hull, protected the turret from being immobilized at its turning base. Armor was about the same as on the M3, but because of contour changes it was more effective.

"By November 1941, manufacture of pilots had started. To get increased production, additional manufacturers were brought into the program.

"Ordnance Committee action in December 1941 provided that a welded hull should be used for Medium Tank M4 and designated the tank with cast hull as Medium Tank M4A1. The pilot Medium Tank T6, under the designation Medium Tank M4A1, was used by Aberdeen Proving Ground for further development and testing in order to eliminate interference and to improve the design of various components and assemblies as follows.

"Combination Gun Mount M34 (T48)

"A pilot model of this mount, for the 75-mm gun and cal. .30 machine gun,

was made by an outside manufacturer and installed in the tank. Such minor defects and interferences as were discovered were corrected in the production mounts.

"The recoil cylinders used for the M34 mount were the same as those used in the M1 mount for the 75-mm Gun M2 on Medium Tank M3. With the 75-mm Gun M3, heavier recoil springs were found to be necessary to bring the gun back to battery when temperatures were below 30deg F or elevations were greater than 25deg. With the heavier recoil springs it was necessary to hold the buffer clearances between 0.003 and 0.004in to obtain proper buffer action.

"A shield was later added to the new gun mount to protect the rotor and cradle from small-caliber fire. This served to keep small-caliber fire from locking the rotor against the front plate, reduced the possibility of bullet splash entering the fighting compartment, and acted as a counterweight that helped to balance the gun and thus aided the operation of the stabilizer.

"Another splash guard, placed on the bottom section of the front plate, further reduced the possibility of bullet splash entering the fighting compartment around the gun rotor.

"Power Traversing Mechanism

"As a result of tests made on power traversing mechanisms for turrets, the Oilgear hydraulics unit was recommended as the standard power traverse for production tanks. The Oilgear Co., however, was not equipped to produce enough units to meet the planned production of tanks, and the Westinghouse electric and Logansport hydraulic units were recommended as substitutes.

"The Oilgear unit was recommended because of its sensitivity of control. Furthermore, since its control was obtained through a variable-stroke, piston-type pump, tight spots in the turret race or ring gear had a relatively minor effect upon the smoothness of operation. Operation of the Westinghouse electric unit and particularly of the Logansport hydraulic unit was noticeably affected by tight spots.

"All of the recommended traversing mechanisms were designed to fit the same mounting bracket in the turret. The hydraulic traversing mechanism used the same gear reduction unit, whereas the

gear reduction unit for the Westinghouse electric traversing mechanism was incorporated in the traversing unit proper. Since the motor of the motor generator set used by the Westinghouse electric traversing mechanism ran at approximately 3,600rpm as compared to 2,000rpm for the hydraulic units, it was necessary to employ two different gyrostabilizer pumps.

"Stowage

"Stowage equipment to be carried in the medium tanks of the M4 series corresponded to that in the M3 series with a few exceptions.

"Because the 75-mm gun was mounted in the turret and required a depression of -12deg, it was not possible to

locate any stowage containers on the front or rear top deck. It was necessary, therefore, to carry most of the equipment inside the fighting compartment.

"All available space inside the fighting compartment was utilized for stowage of either equipment or ammunition, and it was considered that a very satisfactory arrangement was obtained. This was possible only because the stowage problem was given consideration early in the design of the tank.

"Interior Lighting

"Dome lights to give interior lighting of the tank were located on the roof of the turret, on the roof above the right and left sponson, and on the tank front plate.

These lights were equipped with 3-candlepower bulbs. To reduce breakage, plastic lenses were used. [The plastic lenses came in both clear and red for night use when the hatches were open.]

"Tank Seats

"It was necessary to provide adjustable seats for the 75-mm gunner, the driver, and the assistant driver. A standard seat was designed for these three positions which allowed 12in movement up and down and 5in movement fore and aft.

"Because an adjustable seat was not essential for either the 75-mm loader or the tank commander, the standard seats used in the Medium Tank M3 were installed in the pilot model for these two

Posed for pictures on June 9, 1942, is an early M4A1 pilot vehicle. Gone now is the special 75mm gun sight rotor from the top of the turret. Instead, a simpler replaceable periscope fitted with a telescopic sight was used. On the vehicle pictured, the gunner's periscope has been withdrawn into the top of the turret. Also prominent are the direct-vision slots for the driver and assistant driver positions. *US Army*

crew members. Adjustable seats were provided later. [Each seat had a lap strap for safety.]

"Ventilators

"Actual experience and tests with the Medium Tank M3 showed that to exhaust gun gases in the fighting compartment, it was necessary to provide more air intake area in the fighting compartment. This area was obtained by the use of three armored ventilators.

"In the design of the Medium Tank M4 the three armored ventilators were also included, two located in the hull and one in the turret.

"Assistant Driver's Hatch

"The design of the tank was changed to provide an escape hatch for the assistant driver. It was similar to the driver's hatch except that the hatch opened in the opposite direction. It was provided with a periscope with a 200deg field of vision similar to that on the driver's hatch.

"Shield For Cal. .30 Flexible Bow Machine Gun

"The flexible bow gun was mounted in a ball mount that limited the elevation to 25deg. This installation was shielded against locking and bullet splash and allowed ample movement for normal fighting demands.

"Turret Redesign

"The sight rotor for the 75-mm gun was eliminated to avoid the possibility of bullet splash entering this opening and of the gun's being put out of action as a result of a direct hit or from the bullet splash that might freeze the sight rotor. It was replaced by a periscope that extended through the top of the turret and was connected to the gun by a parallel linkage. The thickness of the turret front was increased from 2in to 3in.

"Auxiliary Periscope Design

"The driver and assistant driver were provided with direct-vision slots for use in case their periscopes were shot out. The drawings as released by Aberdeen Proving Ground called for the opening around the hinge of the direct-vision slot to be machined and held to a maximum clearance of 0.010in. The casting manu-

facturers were given permission by the Ordnance Office to core this opening, a method that resulted in clearance of as much as 1/4in between the hull and the hinge of the direct-vision slot. The opening for the direct-vision slot handle when cored through this section of the hull permitted bullet splash to enter the fighting compartment because of the large clearance between the hull and the direct-vision slot hinge. In addition, because of the length of the periscope holder was increased 2in, there was interference between the periscope holder and the driver's and assistant driver's heads. It was therefore difficult to use the direct-vision slot.

"A quick-fix method was designed which prevented bullet splash from entering the fighting compartment. This quick-fix consisted of 3/8in steel plates welded to the inside of the hull around the handle of the direct-vision slot.

"An auxiliary periscope design was prepared for both the cast and the welded hull. The auxiliary periscopes were recommended to replace the direct-vision slots for the following reasons.

"a. Safety of the driver and assistant driver under combat conditions would be increased because bullet splash would be eliminated; resistance to high-explosive and armor-piercing projectiles would be increased; and because if either auxiliary periscope were shot out, neither the driver nor the assistant driver would be injured, as would be the case if a shot entered a direct-vision slot.

"b. The field of vision would be much greater and the interference with the main periscope would be eliminated.

"c. Manufacturing would be greatly simplified."

In 1941, the Army's main concern was that there be no interruption in the production of tanks when the changeover from the M3 to the M4 series was made.

While Chrysler faced the difficult job of switching production from one type of tank to another, the Lima Locomotive Works built the first production M4A1 (cast hull) Sherman for the British. The Sherman rolled off their assembly line in February 1942, four months before Chrysler finished their first production M4 (welded hull) Sherman. In March 1942 the Pressed Steel Car Co. started building

Coming down the production line at the Lima Locomotive Works in early 1942 are a number of M4A1 cast steel hulls. The hulls still have the slots for the fixed, twin .30cal machine guns. These hulls also have the early model three-piece transmission cover, which was bolted together. *US Army*

M4s. Pacific Car and Foundry Co. began building M4s in May of that year.

In 1943, additional companies came on-line to build M4s for varying amounts of time. They included the American Locomotive Co., Baldwin Locomotive Works, Federal Machine and Welder Co., Ford Motor Co., Pullman Standard Manufacturing Co., and the Fisher, Grand Blanc Tank Arsenal. The only companies to build M4s until the end of the war were Chrysler, Fisher Tank Arsenal, and the Pressed Steel Car Co.

Normal sequence in deploying a new tank includes building and field testing a prototype, which is supposed to be functionally finished. Next, manufacturers build pilot models to make sure their tooling can fit all the pieces together on the assembly line. Following the successful testing of pilot tanks, the company produces production models. The Sherman skipped the typical prototype stage and went straight from the pilot tank stage into production.

The lack of extended testing for the prototype M4 meant that the tankers in the field and combat discovered a number of the design problems. As a result, improvements in the Sherman design had to be included as time permitted without upsetting the very high production rates asked for by the US government. During the three years that 75mm-gun-equipped Shermans were built (1942–1944), their turrets and hulls underwent many detail changes.

Much like the famous Model T Ford which came in only one body style and color (black), the first generation of M4s built between 1942 and 1944 came in only one basic body style and mostly one color (olive drab). While Commonwealth allies received over 17,000; the Soviet Army accepted delivery of roughly 4,000.

Lacking the design brilliance and superb armor protection of the Soviet T34 medium tank or the terrific firepower of the German Panther and Tiger tanks, the Sherman made up for it all in its incredible mechanical reliability. Where other tanks of other countries would have littered the roadsides with mechanical breakdowns, the Sherman would plow along. Some Sherman crews used the same tank from the landing on the beaches of Normandy, France, in June 1944 through the end of the war in Europe in

May 1945 without a single major mechanical breakdown.

The first generation of Shermans (M4, M4A1, M4A2, M4A3, M4A4, and M4A6) were armed with the same 75mm main gun. The second generation of upgraded Shermans were fitted with a 76mm main gun. All models of the Sherman featured a cast-steel armored turret mounted on a hull of either cast-steel armor or welded-steel armor plate construction. (Later models of the M4 and M4A6 had a composite hull of both cast- and welded-steel armor construction.) Most Shermans also featured identical transmissions, suspension systems, and tracks. Besides many small items, the principal difference between the various models of first-generation M4s was the engine.

The British military called the M4 the Sherman 1, the M4A1 the Sherman 2, the M4A2 the Sherman 3, the M4A3 the Sherman 4, and the M4A4 the Sherman 5.

The M4 and M4A1 Sherman tanks were powered by Wright (built by Continental) R-975 radial gasoline engines. The M4-model Sherman had a welded-steel armor hull, the M4A1 had a cast-steel armored hull. Between 1942 and 1944, 6,748 M4s and 6,281 M4A1 tanks were built.

The M4A2 was powered by GM twin diesel engines. During the war, 8,053 M4A2 tanks were built. They were used mostly by British forces.

The M4A3, the most popular model among American tankers, was equipped with a Ford V–8 gasoline engine. Armed with the 75mm gun, 4,761 versions of the M4A3 tank were built.

The M4A4, was powered by five in-line 6cyl Chrysler car engines welded together it was known as the A57 multibank engine;. Between 1942 and 1944, 7,499 M4A4s were built. The M4A4 was also widely used by British armored forces.

Last was the M4A6 tank, which was powered by a Caterpillar radial diesel engine. Only 75 were built and never saw field service.

M4s weighed in at about 34 tons combat loaded. They were 9ft 7in tall, 8ft 9in wide and had a length of 20ft 7in. The M4A4 and M4A6 were slightly longer because of their larger engines. Depending on the engine fitted and the

type of terrain being crossed, the average M4 had an operating range of about 100mi, using about one gallon of fuel per mile.

In order to produce the maximum number of tanks during 1942, arrangements were made to manufacture them in Canada. In February 1942, the Ordnance Committee designated the Canadian vehicle as the M4A5. The British designation was RAM II.

These tanks employed the standard M3 tank chassis, with a radial, air-cooled Wright R-975 engine, and a cast upper hull and cast turret. The turret was of the British type, with a radio bulge at the rear, and mounted the main gun. The pilot model had a 2-pounder gun, corresponding to the American 37mm gun. In production vehicles, however, these were replaced by 6-pounder guns, corresponding to American 57mm guns. A small cupola on the left front of the hull roof mounted a .30cal machine gun. A 3in smoke projector was mounted in the right side of the turret front plate. The driver sat at the right side, shifting gears with his left hand. Entrance doors were provided in the right and left sides of the upper hull.

Because American factories began turning out so many Shermans by 1943, it was felt that there was no need for another tank model to be built in Canada. As a result further Ram II production was canceled. Of the roughly 2,000 Ram II tanks built, most were used only as training vehicles in Canada.

Inside the Lima Locomotive Works, employees use an overhead pulley to lower the vehicle's 75mm gun and mantle into the turret of an almost finished M4A1 tank. Lima built 1,655 M4A1 tanks between February 1942 and September 1943. *US Army*

Chapter 2

Armor Protection

Unlike the late-war German tanks, which were designed for maximum firepower and armor protection at the expense of mobility, the Sherman design was based on the concept of mobility, the necessity of overseas shipment, long lines of communications, and the requirement of quantity production, placing firepower and protection on a much lower level of priority. For example, the M4's front hull was 2in thick, with the front of the turret being 3.5in at its thickest. In contrast, the Tiger II front hull was highly sloped and 6in thick with 7.5in of steel armor on the front of the turret.

The sides and rear of the M4 hull were 1.5in thick with the top of the hull being 0.75in thick. Its hull floor varied from 1in at the front (where mine damage was most likely) to 0.5in at the rear of the hull plate. The sides and rear of the Sherman

Beneath the visible part of the Sherman tank turret was the turret basket. The turret basket rotated with the turret and formed a floor for the turret crew to stand on. On this particular vehicle, a large truck-mounted crane removes the turret.

turret were 2in thick and 1in thick on the top.

An early pilot model of an M4A1 tank built by the Pacific Car and Foundry Company poses at Aberdeen Proving Ground in June 1942. The direct-vision slots for the driver and assistant driver are located on the front hull of the tank. Sherman tanks were 9ft 10in tall , they typically weighed in at about 34 tons. Pacific Car and Foundry Company built 926 M4A1 Shermans during World War II. *US Army*

Hull

Unlike the automobile, which consists of a separate chassis and body joined together, a tank hull is a one-piece body constructed of armor plates of varying thickness, depending upon location. The hull is normally designed to be as small as possible to reduce both the vehicle's height and weight, yet at the same time it must house the crew and the vehicle's engine, powertrain, ammunition, and other operating equipment.

On Shermans, the engines were mounted at the rear of the hull in a compartment separated from the fighting compartment by a thin armored bulkhead. The cooling system, fuel tanks, and the gasoline tank for the auxiliary generator engine were filled from the top of the hull on the right and left sides at the rear of the turret.

Each filler opening was marked with a metal plate having raised letters so that they could be readily identified even in the dark. Two heavy louvered covers over the compartment allowed access to the engine compartment. The covers also served as the main inlet for the cooling air. Between the engine or engines and the louvered covers was a splash guard hinged at the front so that it could be raised to give access to the engine. A support was attached to the underside of the splash panel to hold in the raised position.

All M4s were fitted with a fire-extinguisher system. The system consisted of two fixed 10lb bottles of carbon dioxide clamped to the vehicle's bulkhead at the left of the turret fighting compartment. In case of fire, the bottles squirted carbon dioxide into the vehicle's engine compartment. The fire extinguisher system could be actuated from the inside of the vehicle by reaching down from the turret to physically pull the handles on the bottles. They could also be actuated from behind the driver's position. On the outside of the Sherman, an escaped crew member or surrounding infantrymen could use a T-handle to actuate the system. Two portable extinguishers were also part of the fire extinguisher system. One was located in the vehicle's turret and the other near the driver in the front hull.

The Sherman had a 24vdc electrical system with a belt from the propeller shaft driving a 50amp main generator. Inside the Sherman's hull was an auxiliary generator unit nicknamed Little Joe. It was a two-cycle, single-cylinder generator that generated 24vdc. Little Joe was used to charge the vehicle batteries and aid in starting the vehicle. It was also used through some adjustable ducts to provide heat to both the engine and crew compartments. It was also helpful if the Sherman had to stand still for a couple of days, to keep batteries charged for monitoring radios. The auxiliary generator had its own separate fuel tank that could hold 5gal of fuel, enough to run the generator for about 12hr.

A pair of driving lights, protected from damage by steel brackets, were normally fitted to the front of all Sherman hulls. Above and attached to the driving lights were blackout position lights. If needed, the crew could also use a spotlight attached to 15ft of extension cord. Since bullets or shell fragments could easily destroy the driving lights, Sherman crews could remove them from the front hull for safekeeping.

Located on top of the Sherman hull (depending on the model) were at least two armored ventilators. They ventilated the powder gases that built up inside the vehicle's hull from the firing of the 75mm main gun or machine guns. An armored

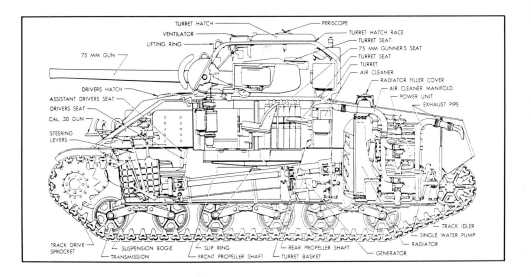

A sectional view of a diesel-powered M4A4 Sherman tank shows its various components and their locations in the vehicle. Most diesel-powered Shermans were supplied to America's wartime allies, especially the British Army. *US Army*

ventilator was also mounted on its turret. At the rear of the hull were engine air intakes.

On top of the Sherman hull were four heavy-duty lifting brackets, used in loading and unloading the vehicle by crane into transport ships. The Sherman's lower front and lower rear hull had towing handles lugs.

While Sherman crews might pile an incredible amount of their personal belongings on top of their vehicles, the normal attachments consisted of a number of large tools, such as a sledgehammer and a track adjusting wrench. Also draped over the vehicle's hull was a towing cable.

The strangest item fitted to the front hull of most Shermans was a siren. The siren alerted other vehicles or troops in the rear area that tanks were approaching their position. It was also used in combat as a signaling device.

Emergency Escape Hatch

On the bottom of the Sherman hull was an emergency escape hatch. It was located behind the assistant driver's seat and was secured by four bolts, all of which were connected to a single control lever for quick release.

The normal method for entering or leaving any tank is by climbing in or out through its top hatches located in the turret and front hull. In combat, when a Sherman was hit and it was necessary to leave the vehicle, the crew was occasionally forced by small arms fire to climb out of the bottom emergency hatch. In combat, tank crews leaving a damaged or destroyed vehicle are considered important targets. Normally, machine-gun fire from opposing tanks or infantry would be used to kill the tank crews as they tried to leave their vehicles.

Lt. Col. Henry Gardiner, who commanded both M4 and M3 tanks in North Africa, experienced both sides of the common wartime practice of gunning down tank crews when they were forced to leave their vehicles. In a 1943 letter to his wife, Gardiner describes a battle between his unit (he was commanding an M3 Lee at the time) and German forces on December 3, 1942.

"Cocke and I decided to return and see what had happened to the rest of our force. We again drew fire while we were proceeding across the flat and his tank was hit and burned but everyone escaped without injury. There were no tanks in the olive grove when we reached it but they had all pulled back to the vicinity of Tebourba, many of them having taken shelter in and around the buildings. Some shells were coming in and most everyone had taken cover.

"After some difficulty I got them out of the various positions they had taken

Very early on, a stronger one-piece casting replaced the Sherman tank's original three-piece differential housing. On the bottom of the differential housing are two towing brackets. *US Army*

This picture shows the smooth contours of the M4A1 cast hull. The photo was taken during a training exercise in the United States during the war. Notice the soldiers carried on the vehicle's rear engine deck. This was not normal practice in the US Army, since most soldiers accompanying tank units were provided with armored troop carriers. *US Army*

and deployed them into line and we started out over the broad hill between Tebourba and the enemy. We drew some fire. As tanks began to appear in the distance, I ordered ours to fire on them. Our tanks showed a hesitancy to advance and a movement forward was largely accomplished by my moving ahead fifty or one hundred yards and then their coming up parallel to me.

"On one such move I suddenly discovered a German tank below me at a distance of about 300 yards. Since I had used up all my 75, I ordered my 37 gunner to fire an AP [armor piercing] and he scored a hit the first shot. Had him put in another and then the crew started to crawl out and run away from it, whereupon I ordered him to cut loose with his machine-gun. This caused them to turn around and run back so as to secure the protection of their tank."

In a letter to his father, Gardiner wrote about the Germans destroying his tanks in combat and then shooting at him and his crew as they tried to escape from the burning vehicles.

"I am sorry that the War Department's announcement to you was worded as it was because I certainly was not seriously wounded although I might well have been since two of the boys in my tank were killed and two seriously wounded. When you get a hit on a tank that knocks it out, the results are apt to be pretty serious for the occupants. If they don't get you in the tank, they do their best as you are leaving it. Had another tank knocked out about ten days ago in which one of the crew was killed and another seriously wounded. Those of us who got away did so under a perfect hail of bullets. We ran a short distance but concluded it was too hot so fell down and crawled for about three hundred yards before we decided we could get on our feet again. I was helping a wounded boy and the enemy tanks caught up to us and I had to leave him and make another break for it which was also under fire. Formed a very poor opinion of their marksmanship that day.

"Had quite an experience since I lay in an exposed position with enemy tanks passing on both sides of me until darkness fell which was the longest hour of my life to date. I then made a wide circuit through the hills and hiked between thirty and thirty-five miles back to our own lines. That experience seemed to have interested some of the gentlemen of the press so you may read some version of it. I always give them Chicago as my ad-

24

dress since that is where my military records list me as coming from."

The Sherman's emergency escape hatch was also used on numerous occasions to pick up wounded soldiers. From the book *Tanks are Mighty Fine Things* comes this story by Marine Corps Pfc. Frank Upton who was fighting the Japanese on Tinian Island in 1944.

"I love tanks and everybody connected with them. When I was hit in Tinian we were on patrol and the Nips had pinned us down in a field of sugar cane. They were in caves in the cliffs and while we could see exactly nothing of them, they were really giving us the business. A machine gun slug went through my hip early and I had visions of being in the field until dark when one of those Chrysler jobs [Sherman] rolled up. The driver told me what he was going to do and after I had crawled out on harder ground, he drove the tank over me and pulled me through the escape hatch in the belly of the tank. Those threads looked plenty big as they straddled me, but we drove back to the lines slick as a whistle."

When front-line Sherman units pulled into an overnight position that might be subject to enemy artillery or mortar fire, crews often dug slit trenches in which the crew could take turns sleeping. To protect themselves from the enemy shell fire, the tanks drove over the slit trenches giving them 34 tons of overhead steel protection. (You could sleep in an M4 if desperate enough, but due to the cramped nature of all tanks, staying in one for extended periods of time can get uncomfortable.)

When dug in under their Shermans, the tank crews used the emergency escape hatch as their means of entrance and exit from the vehicle so as to not expose themselves to any outside artillery or mortar fire. For company or battalion commanders sleeping under their vehicles, the tank's radios could be run down into the occupant's slit trench through the escape hatch so that the commander could maintain constant contact with any orders from higher headquarters' units.

Turret

Located in the middle of the Sherman hull was the vehicle's power-operated three-man turret. Access was provided by either one or two hatches.

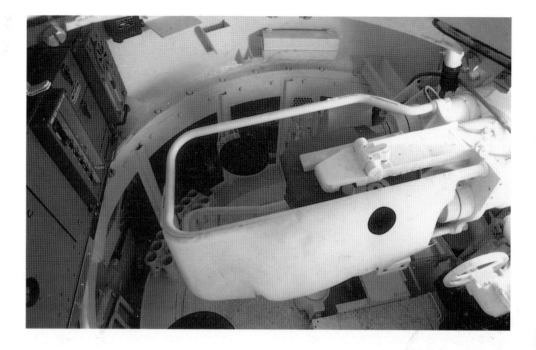

Looking down through the commander's hatch of an M4A1 Sherman into the turret compartment. Both the tank commander's and loader's seats are visible. The gunner's seat is missing from this particular vehicle. In the rear of the turret is the vehicle's radio.

The large white-painted object in the turret's middle is a body guard. It protects the turret crew personnel from getting too close to the 75mm main gun when the gun is fired and the recoil pushes the gun's breech to the rearward position. *Michael Green*

The three men located in the Sherman turret were the tank commander, who had a hatch right above him; the gunner, who sat below and in front of the commander; and the loader, who sat or stood on the turret's left side. In some model Shermans, the loader and gunner both had to leave the vehicle through the tank commander's hatch. In peacetime, this wasn't a problem. In combat, however, it was a different story because the Sherman burned so easily and so fast when hit by enemy antitank weapons. Many Sherman gunners and especially loaders burned to death before they could escape their vehicles. Most later model Shermans provided another turret hatch cover over the loader's position to give that person easy access in and out of the turret.

Beneath the visible part of the Sherman turret was the turret basket. This lower section of the turret, which sat inside the hull turret ring, rotated with the turret and formed a floor for the turret crew to stand on. Later model Shermans deleted the turret basket; the turret crew sat on seats attached to the turret itself.

The turret ring is the circular opening in the hull roof of a tank in which the turret bearing race fits. The wider the turret ring, the larger the turret that can be fitted; and the larger the turret normally means the larger the gun that can be mounted in it.

All Sherman models were fitted with a turret bustle, which was nothing more than an extension on the rear of the turret allowing room for radios and providing more space for the recoil of the tank's main gun. The bustle also counterbalances the gun weight making it easier to turn the turret when the vehicle is on a slope.

Many Shermans were fitted with a British-developed smoke grenade launcher, much like a signaling flare system. The device was mounted in Sherman turrets on the loader's side at a fixed angle. The rear of the device hinged in two, allowing the loader to load a smoke grenade or flare. The only aiming control over the launcher unit was by traversing the entire Sherman turret in the direction you wanted to fire it. There was no elevation control for the unit.

Armor

Like all tanks of World War II, the Sherman was protected by high-strength, heat-treated steel armor. Steel armor is composed of a small amount of carbon and various other alloy elements, the main ones being nickel and chromium.

The Sherman hull was built out of either welded-steel armor plates or cast steel or a combination of both types.

Cast-steel armor first appeared on the turrets of the French designed and built Renault FT-17 light tank during World War I. Casting steel armor had its advantages. Some shapes are best made by casting (for example tank turrets, because of their intricate curves). The original T6 pilot model of the Sherman featured a cast-steel armor hull.

The Sherman was built by a number of different companies, some of which did not have the ability to produce large castings. The building of welded-hull Shermans, therefore, was seen as a viable alternative for companies without the equipment or skill to cast objects as large as a tank hull. Unfortunately, welding Sherman hulls together was much more labor intensive than casting. More labor meant more cost.

The M4-model Sherman had a welded-steel armor hull and the M4A1 Sherman had a cast-steel armor hull. Because of its more boxlike shape, the M4 with the welded-steel armor hull had a bit more interior stowage space. All M4 models through the post-war years featured cast-steel armor turrets.

The M4A1 with its more rounded cast-steel armor hull was supposed to be better at deflecting enemy antitank weapons than the more boxlike welded-hull M4s. Generally, however, castings do not always have the strength or hardness of rolled-steel plates. Because of the difficul-

An excellent comparison photo of the two different types of Sherman hulls. The vehicle on the left is an M4A1 with the rounded, cast-steel hull. On the lower front hull the vehicle is fitted with the famous Cullin hedgerow device used to push through the thick hedges of the French countryside in June and July 1944. The vehicle on the right is an M4 with the more boxlike welded-steel armor hull. The M4 is armed with a 105mm howitzer, instead of the standard 75mm gun, and is referred to as the M4E5 model in this configuration. *US Army*

ty of giving equally uniform heat treatment (hardening) in the production of cast armor, sometimes the armor's ballistic properties suffered. At least one tank unit was convinced of the strength of welded-steel Shermans and would not use any others. Most Sherman tankers didn't really care, since most enemy anti-tank weapons could shoot through the armor of any Sherman at almost any range.

In contrast to the high boxlike shape of the M4 series, the German Army had fielded tanks with thick frontal armor inclined at more than 55deg from the verti-cal. The effectiveness of armor is greatly enhanced (up to double) by sloping it because projectiles tend to bounce off or to shatter on impact. While the famous Tiger I tank was built of vertical steel armor plates, the Tiger made up for its lack of sloped armor by featuring thick armor plates, something the Sherman was never designed to carry.

The Sherman's armor lack of effectiveness is described by Sgt. Harold S. Rathburn, tank commander, in a wartime report.

"In comparing the German tank with our own medium tank, there is one thing that I would like to bring out; that is, the armor plate on each tank. The Mark V [Panther] has about 4 inches on the front. The Mark VI [Tiger] has a little over 6 inches. When placing tank against tank, you must consider the armor of each. In past engagements with the enemy, we have placed tank against tank very often. In one tank battle, our M4 was hit in the front by an AP shell from a Mark VI [Tiger]. It went in the front and came out the rear. I have also seen our 75mm AP shells bounce off the front of the Mark V and Mark VI tanks."

Pfc. Francis P. Kennedy, tanker, describes a combat action involving his Sherman in a wartime report.

"We were hit four times by a 152mm ground mount gun (artillery gun). The first shot between the track and hull on the left side of the tank under the radio tender's position went completely through and broke the right track. The second shot hit the left side where the name of the tank appeared, pierced the left side and exploded inside, setting the tank on fire. The third hit the left sponson, piercing the armor there and coming out again through the other side near the USA W number. It went completely in one side and caused a gaping hole coming out the other side. The fourth hit in the identical spot, but did not come all the way through."

A German Panther tank on display at Aberdeen Proving Ground, Maryland, shows the thick well-sloped frontal armor that made it such a difficult tank to destroy in combat. The given thickness of tank armor is effectively doubled when properly sloped at more than 55deg from the vertical. Approximately 5,000 Panther tanks were built as compared to almost 50,000 Sherman tanks produced by American factories during the war. *Michael Green*

The lack of confidence in the armor protection fitted to the Sherman is best described by an inside joke among American tankers during the war. The joke stated that if you took a hammer or helmet and hit the side of an M4, it was guaranteed that the vehicle's crew would jump out of the vehicle before you could strike the tank a second time.

For Sherman tankers who managed to live through their tank's destruction, the psychological effects proved to be very serious. The Army found out that the typi-cal tanker could stand two or three tanks being destroyed under him before suffering a mental breakdown. A few stood up to six or eight Shermans being destroyed under them without being psychological-ly effected. This only happened, howev-er, when two or three of their vehicles were destroyed in the same day.

There were numerous reasons for the lack of heavier armor not being fitted to the Sherman. Armor is the heaviest element of any tank design. Steel armor plate 1in thick weighs 40lb/sq-ft. When the Sherman was being developed, the engineers designing the vehicle were constrained because existing cranes fitted to most transport ships couldn't load or unload anything heavier than roughly 35 tons. Portable bridges employed by the US Army in the early days of the war were not designed to carry the weight of larger and heavier tanks.

Because of the need to produce a tank with a turret-mounted 75mm gun as fast as possible, the M3 medium tank chassis and engine were used as the basis for the Sherman. While this decision certainly sped up the Sherman's design and pro-duction, it saddled the Sherman builders with a number of design problems. The volute spring suspension system found on the early Shermans was descended from the M2 light tank, but was built larger and heavier. As a result, the chassis of the Sherman was close to its weight-carrying capacity when it was built.

When the Sherman was originally conceived, the main antitank gun of the German army was the 37mm antitank gun (fitted to its Mark IIIs). With an effective range of 600yd, the 37mm antitank gun fired an AP round at 2,625fps. This antitank gun size was also used by the Italian, Japanese, Soviet, French, and American armies in the early days of the war. It was the standard antitank gun of its day and was what American tank designers felt the Sherman needed to be protected against.

American tank designers failed to foresee the amazing advances in antitank-gun

28

technology made by the German Army during the war. While many attempts were made to provide additional armor protection as the war progressed, the Sherman remained badly underprotected.

Because the Sherman was rushed so quickly into production and then into combat, there had been little time to conduct trials on the vehicle to test the effectiveness of its armor protection. In 1942–1943, combat experience in North Africa, where American and British Shermans had gone up against German tanks and antitank weapons, had shown that a considerable number of Shermans were lost because of ammunition fires inside the vehicles.

So bad was the problem of fires inside the tanks that the Germans nicknamed the British-employed Shermans the Tommy Cooker (Tommy was slang for British soldier). American soldiers nicknamed their Shermans Ronsons (the Ronson was a small portable hand-held cigarette lighter of the day, "Guaranteed to light first time," as an advertising of the day claimed).

To protect the hull-mounted 75mm ammunition stowage racks (the Sherman had three) from being set off by enemy projectiles or fragments entering the vehicle, sections of 1in steel armor plate were welded to the outside of both cast and welded Sherman hulls opposite the upper hull interior ammunition stowage racks. This extra armor plate increased the protection for the single rack on the left side of the tank as well as the two on the right.

In some early production M4s, part of the interior turret wall in front of the gunner's position had been machined away to provide more room for the gunner when operating his gun controls. Combat experience, however, showed this to have been a serious mistake. As a result, a number of early model Shermans were fitted with add-on armor plate on the right front of the turret.

These temporary solutions to protect certain areas of the Sherman were deleted when later production turrets and hulls were redesigned with thicker armor in both the hull and turret areas on some Sherman models. The M4 composite hull Sherman did retain the extra add-on hull armor throughout its production life.

Combat experience had shown that the driver's and assistant driver's hatch hoods, which protruded from the front of welded-hull Shermans (M4, M4A2,

The thin, boxlike steel armor of the M4A1 Sherman tank offered little protection for its crew. Hit by an unknown type of enemy weapon, this vehicle suffered a catastrophic explosion, which blew the turret clear off the hull. Such destruction usually occurred when an enemy antitank round entered the tank's hull or turret and set off the vehicle's ammunition. In cases like this, it is unlikely that any crew member survived. *Fred Ropkey collection*

M4A3, and M4A4), were a weak point in deflecting enemy projectiles. While the front of the early model welded-hull Shermans had an excellent 56deg slope to it, the hatch hoods were almost vertical and consequently afforded less protection to the front hull. The rare enemy projectiles that may have been deflected by the front hull's slope would slide up the hull and impact on the almost boxlike hatch hoods and tear them off. The cast-hull Shermans (M4A1 or later M4A6) didn't have this problem because their front hulls had no such bullet traps.

To correct the weak point formed by the hatch hoods on welded-hull Shermans, a new front hull was designed in 1943 to obtain more uniform protection in that area. The new front hull plate (known in military terms as a glacis plate) was inclined (sloped) at 47deg instead of the former 56deg. To make up for the lessened slope angle, the new plate was 2.5in rather than 2in thick.

Larger hatches for the driver and assistant driver were also provided when the welded hulls were redesigned. The earlier hatches were narrow and forced all but the thinnest individual to twist and turn sideways before lowering themselves into the front hull. They also made it difficult to escape rapidly when the tank was hit.

The Army had also developed field kits for adding extra armor to M4A3 welded-hull Shermans with the new 47deg front plates. These full-width, one-piece, 1in-thick steel armor plates covered everything from the top of the front hull all the way to the cast front mounted transmission housing. Prior to these kits, many tankers in Europe had cut off the top half of the front hull plates of destroyed Shermans and attached them to the front hull of their own vehicles. Although the Army-supplied field kits had been designed for only the flat front hulls of the M4A3s these armor-upgrade kits were often applied to M4A1s with the rounded, cast-armor hull.

Other parts of the Sherman that were

uparmored included the vehicle's front differential and final drive. On early model Shermans, they were protected by only 2in of steel armor. Later production models were fitted with a new 4.5in thick steel casting.

Early production models of the Sherman were fitted with a 1sq-ft armored, hinged, pistol port on the left turret wall. Designed as a way for tank crews to use their on-board small arms or grenades against close enemy infantry, American tankers tended to use the pistol port as a handy way to dispose of empty 75mm main gun shell cases instead of letting them pile up on the turret floor. Normally, to get rid of empty 75mm shell cases, the crew threw them out the top-mounted loader's or commander's hatch.

Because the pistol port on the Sherman turret was a weak spot in terms of ballistic protection, in early 1943 the Army ordered them removed from all Shermans in production. Battle experience showed that the port was necessary after all. By early 1944, the pistol port was again placed into the production line.

To compound the problem of inadequate armor, the Sherman was too tall. The lower the tank height, the harder the tank becomes to see on the battlefield and therefore the harder to hit. Both the German and Soviet armies had seen this as a critical element of their tank designs. Unfortunately, the height of the Sherman was dictated by both the narrow width of the M3 medium tank chassis that it inherited and the space required by the radial air-cooled aircraft engines and its front-mounted transmission.

The Sherman turret's height was also controlled by the size of its 75mm gun and the minimum depression specified for the gun. Tank turrets like the Sherman are also governed by the need for the loader to stand and load main gun rounds. According to Capt. Henry W. Johnson of Co. F, 66th Armored Regiment (AR) in a field report, the Sherman's height was a definite disadvantage.

"The silhouette of the Sherman tank is such that it is easily spotted 2,000 to 3,000 yards away. The silhouette presented by the Sherman is far more perpendicular than that of the German Mark V and Mark VI tanks.... It is my opinion that the silhouette presented by the...German tanks is far superior to that presented by our Sherman tank."

Early combat experiences with Sherman tanks in North Africa showed the US Army that the vehicle was too thinly armored. As a short-term solution, the Army had a number of 1in thick steel armor plates welded onto both the hull and turret of early model Sherman tanks. These factory modifications were later dropped when newer production vehicles had been redesigned with thicker armor in certain key areas. The vehicles pictured are somewhere in England in March 1944. The add-on armor plates can be seen both on the hull and turrets of the parked tanks. *US Army*

German Weaponry

The Sherman was vulnerable to an entire host of German antitank weapons ranging from hand-held rocket launchers to the 88mm guns mounted on the Tiger tank. Lt. Col. Wilson M. Hawkins, commander of the 3rd Tank Battalion (TB), 67th AR wrote the following wartime report.

"Our M4 tank does not compare favorably with the German Mark V (Panther tank) or VI (Tiger I tank) in armor plate. Theirs is much thicker than ours and sloped so as to prevent strikes against it at angles approaching the normal. I have inspected the battlefield at Faid Pass in Tunisia, being with the force which retook it. Inspection of our tanks destroyed there indicated that the 88mm gun penetrated into the turret from the front and out again in the rear. Few gouges were found indicating that all strikes had made penetrations. Our tanks were penetrated by 88, 75, and 50mm caliber in this engagement in all parts of the hull and turret. I personally measured many of the holes."

Panzerfaust and Panzerschreck

One of the most common antitank weapons faced by M4s in 1944–1945 was the Panzerfaust (armor fist). The Panzerfaust was the first disposable, recoilless, one-man, antitank weapon fielded in military use. It consisted of an explosive projectile, launch tube, and firing mechanism. Normally used by German soldiers in teams of two or three, the Panzerfaust had a shaped charge warhead and could burn a hole through 8in of steel armor. Easy to use and built in large numbers, the Panzerfaust was only accurate at close ranges.

Before the Panzerfaust, the German Army had built another man-portable antitank weapon known as the Panzerschreck (armor terror). Basically, it was an upscaled copy of a captured American bazooka. Over 300,000 Panzerschrecks were made before the Panzerfaust replaced them in production. The Panzer-

In a little French town in November 1944, this very early model M4A1 cast-hull Sherman tank took two large-caliber antitank rounds into its front hull. The two rounds passed clean through the transmission housing into the vehicle's lower hull area. On many occasions German high-velocity antitank rounds would travel clean through one side of a Sherman tank and out the other. *US Army*

schreck served until the end of the war.

American tankers' impression of these weapons can be found in a field report by Capt. John B. Roller, Jr., of Co. A, 66th AR.

"On 17th day of March 1945 I conducted experiments on a burned American M4 tank to determine the relative penetrating power of the American bazooka, the German bazooka, and the German Panzerfaust. I found that at 100 yards all of these weapons penetrated the tank, but in each case the hole made by the German weapon was made greater than that made by the American. In a hit on the turret I found that the American bazooka made a very small hole, approximately 1/2-inch in diameter. As compared with this, the German bazooka made a hole at least one inch in diameter and the Panzerfaust a hole two and three-fourths inches in diameter.

"In my mind there is considerable doubt as to whether the American bazooka would have caused any material damage to the tank or to the crew. On the other hand, the German bazooka would have been much more destructible to both the tank and the crew. I do not believe that any man in the turret would have survived, had the crew been present when the Panzerfaust hit."

For American tankers, facing the Panzerfaust in combat was a hair-raising experience. The following narrative is from the files of the 5th Armored Division (AD). The author is unknown but has managed to capture the urgency, tone, drama, and suspense of the occasion.

Moments after being hit by an enemy anti-tank weapon, this Sherman's onboard ammunition has already started to burn. When hit, a Sherman tank crew had about five seconds or less to get out of their vehicle before it started to burn. Many Sherman-tank veterans remember the horrible screams on the radio of their fellow tankers whose tanks had been hit by enemy fire and then burned to death because they failed to get out of their vehicles in time. Thankfully for everybody's nerves, the radios in tanks that were hit usually ceased operation fairly quickly. *US Army*

"The column sailed along for the first three miles the morning of April 2 and then the Germans struck hard. As the leading tank neared a road block, a ten-foot long tongue of flame lashed from a building beside the road. A black, bulbous object came hurtling like a football toward one of the tanks. It slammed into the side and exploded with a blinding flash. The tank began to burn.

"'Bazooka players,' the other tankers yelled. Another football skimmed past, missed, exploded twenty yards beyond. 'Kill the sons o' bitches,' the tank commanders yelled. Infantrymen hit the ditch, started blazing with their rifles at Germans sticking their heads out of foxholes. It was a showdown between the tank-infantry teams and the German Panzerfaust, a $4.00 bazooka which can knock out one of our $60,000 tanks and kill all five of the crew. The only hope of our tanks and infantry was to scare the hell out of the Germans so they couldn't shoot straight.

"Every cannon and every machine gun on every tank opened up. Doughboys poured in furious fire from the ditches and nothing above ground could live in the face of the combined blast. A German raised up, fired his Panzerfaust and then threw up his hands in surrender. A tank machine gun chopped him up. He had surrendered too late. Other Jerries, afraid to look over the top of their holes, stuck their Panzerfausts up above the surface of the ground and fired wildly, sending 'footballs' harmlessly through the air. Several krauts jumped out and tried to run, but they didn't get far. The infantry moved in with bayonets and soon everything was quiet."

Besides using intensive fire to force the Panzerfaust gunners to keep their heads down, M4 crews developed a number of other defensive measures to reduce the effectiveness of the Panzerfaust. A field-expedient way to beef up the Sherman's thin armor was to find spare tracks, sandbags, wooden logs, planks, chicken wire, and any other materials and secure them to the Sherman. These additional items acted as a standoff from the armor to detonate the warheads of the Panzerfaust before they actually struck the vehicle's armor. It didn't always work that way, but it worked often enough to convince many Sherman crews to load down their vehicles with a wide variety of different materials. An example of the effectiveness of this add-on material is described in a wartime report.

"T/Sgt. Heyd, Maintenance Sergeant of Co. E 67th AR has seen and retrieved all tanks of this company which had been hit by enemy tank and anti-tank guns. Of a total of 19 tanks hit, 17 tanks had been penetrated while only 2 tanks had withstood the force of the enemy high-velocity shells and ricocheted. These ricochets were due to the added protection of sand bags and logs used to reinforce the armor plate in front of the tank."

Antitank Mines

Another worry for M4 crews was the antitank mine. Almost 16 percent (more in certain areas) of American tanks were lost to antitank mines during the war.

The Germans normally used antitank mines to beef up defensive positions. Mine fields could either completely stop a formation of M4s or channel the American tanks into an area where the Germans had preplanned an ambush with other antitank weapons.

Most antitank mines are comprised of a large explosive charge coupled to a pressure-sensitive firing device. When an M4 drove over the mine, the resulting explosion normally broke a track and damaged various parts of the suspension system. If the Sherman lost its mobility, it quickly fell prey to other German anti-tank weapons.

An example of what mines could do to a US Army offensive is recounted by Maj. W. M. Daniel, executive officer of an M4 battalion, in a combat interview report of the 5th AD fighting in the Hurtgen Forest in late 1944.

"Shoulders of the roads where engineers had worked were thick with anti-tank and anti-personnel mines. They found enemy and American personnel dead. The enemy had cleared out before the tanks and infantry arrived. The force was limited to the depth it could get off the road. There was no fire of consequence as they went up. One round fell in front of tank CP. One man was hit by artillery or mortar fire. At a point near Kleinhau, a supply of 81 and 120mm mortar shells were found.

"The force was so channeled to roads that it was difficult to operate. This made for an almost impossible situation since there was a winding road to the left of the town. The force was exposed once it got past the edge of the woods. Tanks normally can give a shield of armor to dismounted infantry, but in many cases here it was impossible to do this because of mines."

Antitank Guns

The German Army introduced a 50mm antitank gun (Pak 38) in the spring of 1941 (the same time the Sherman was being developed) to replace the 37mm antitank gun. The 50mm antitank gun was mounted on a split-trail two-wheel carriage and was normally towed by a half-track vehicle. It could fire two types of AP rounds: solid shot round and another one armed with a tungsten carbide core which had a muzzle velocity of

3,940fps. Both of these rounds could penetrate the armor on the Sherman. The Pak 38 was the standard antitank gun used by the Germans in North Africa.

In 1942 the German Army began fielding a 75mm towed antitank gun known as the Pak 40. Looking much like a scaled-up version of the older 50mm antitank gun, the 75mm Pak 40 was the most numerous threat faced by Shermans in Europe. The Panther tank mounted a heavier, more powerful 75mm cannon known as the Kwk 42.

The best-known Sherman killer was the famous German 88mm gun. Originally developed in the 1920s, the 88mm started out strictly as an antiaircraft gun, but in North Africa, the Germans soon realized its effectiveness as an antitank weapon and developed two tank cannons from the 88mm, which they mounted on a number of tanks and tank destroyers. The 88mm gun was also mount-

An American soldier of the 5th AD surveys the results of accurate German antitank fire. This Sherman has been subjected to serious internal explosions that have left the turret ajar. On the back of the turret is the stowed position for the .50cal machine gun. *US Army*

ed in small numbers on a towed antitank mount.

The 88mm gun mounted on the German Tiger I tank had a muzzle velocity of 3,000fps. The 88mm gun in the Tiger II fired a round that weighed almost 23lb and traveled approximately 3,340fps.

S/Sgt. Lewis Kuch of the 2nd AD talks about the German 88mm gun in a report.

"The German 88 AT gun is by far the best gun on the battlefield today. It's a long range and high-velocity gun, which enables it to fire on our tanks at such a range that it is almost worthless to shoot back, even if we are able. The gun is equipped with muzzle-break, which helps a lot. The powder charge is a smokeless type, which is in their favor also. No smoke—and it's hard to tell where it comes from."

Col. Erling J. Foss, communications officer for the 5th AD, during the war, remembers visiting a field in Holland where a platoon of five Shermans had bedded down for the night. Unbeknownst to them, they had parked themselves right in front of a dug-in Tiger tank. The Tiger tank fired one shot from its 88mm gun that went through one side and out the other of one Sherman and continued on through one side and out the other side of another Sherman parked 50yd away parallel to the first.

By August and September 1944, the Allied forces managed to break out of the original landing areas and the dense hedgerow-dominated countryside of Normandy. With the German Army on the run and complete air superiority, the M4's thin armor protection was quietly forgotten. When an occasional German tank was encountered, the Sherman quickly broke contact and maneuvered to attack from the flank where even the Panther and Tiger tanks were vulnerable to a shot from the Sherman's 75mm or 76mm cannon. At this time, the German Mark IV was still the most numerous tank in the German Army service, and the most likely vehicle the Sherman encountered in combat.

The Sherman disadvantage in armor protection was noticed again in late 1944 as a wet winter set in. The Allied armies were closer to the German border and more German heavy tanks appeared. The poor weather conditions severely cut back on air cover that had made up for the M4's lack of firepower. Wet and muddy terrain forced the M4s to remain on the roads and denied them mobility. The M4s were forced to deal with German antitank weapons and tanks in head-on duels.

Sgt. Chester J. Marczak sums up the feelings of many Sherman crewmen in the following narrative from a wartime report.

"The German's high-velocity guns and souped-up ammunition can penetrate our thickest armor. At a range where it would be suicide for us to shoot, they shoot. What we need is more armor, higher velocity, not necessarily a bigger

gun, souped-up ammunition, and a means whereby we can maneuver faster, making sharper turns. I've seen many times when the air force was called out to wipe out scattered tanks rather than letting our tanks get slaughtered.

"All of us know that the German tanks are far superior to anything that we have in combat. They are able to maneuver on a space the length of their tank. How can we outflank them when all they have to do is pivot and keep their frontal armor toward us? Their frontal armor is practically invulnerable to our 75's, except at an exceptionally close range—and they never let us get that close.

The very prominent hatch hoods of the early welded-hull Sherman tanks can be seen on this Canadian Army vehicle nicknamed *Vancouver*. Because of the nearly vertical surface presented by these hatch hoods, they were a weak point in deflecting enemy antitank rounds. *Canadian Army*

We've got a good tank—for parades and training purposes—but for combat they are just potential coffins. I know! I've left them burning after the first few rounds of German shells penetrated our thickest armor."

Sherman crews in Europe quickly lost heart. As morale began to suffer, the at-

An overhead view of the very narrow driver's hatch found on early Sherman tanks. These poorly designed hatches were difficult to get out of in a hurry. In front of the driver's hatch hood is a welded-on 1in steel armor plate designed to upgrade the driver's armor. *Michael Green*

tention of American reporters was awakened. Hanson Baldwin wrote the following sentiments in *The New York Times* in January 1945.

"Why at this late stage in the war are American tanks inferior to the enemy's? That they are inferior the fighting in Normandy showed, and the recent battles in Ardennes have again emphatically demonstrated. This has been denied, explained away and hushed up, but the men who are fighting our tanks against much heavier, better armored and more powerfully armed German monsters know the truth. It is high time that Congress got to the bottom of a situation that does no credit to the War Department. This does not mean that our tanks are bad. They are not; they are good. They are the best tanks in the world—next to the Germans."

In response to mounting criticism in the American press, Gen. George Patton defended the Sherman design. The March 31, 1945, issue of *The Army and Navy Journal* published the following letter.

"Lieutenant General George S. Patton, Jr., Commanding General of the Third Army, has replied to criticism that American tanks are not comparable with German Armor in a letter to General Thomas T. Handy, deputy chief of staff.

"Following are excerpts from the letter, written from Third Army headquarters under date of 19 March.

"'It has come to my knowledge that certain misguided or perhaps deliberately mendacious individuals, returning from the theater of war, have criticized the equipment of the American soldier. I have been in command of fighting units since the 7th of November 1942, and may therefore claim some knowledge of the various types of equipment.

"'With reference to the tank, either M5 (light) or M4 (medium), it has been stated at home that these tanks are not comparable with the German Panther and Tiger type tanks. This statement is wholly incorrect for several reasons.

"'Since 1 August 1944, when the Third Army became operational, our total tank casualties have amounted to 1136 tanks. During the same period we have accounted for 2287 German tanks, of which 808 were of the Tiger or Panther variety, and 851 on our side were M4. These figures of themselves refute any inferiority of our tanks, but let me add that the Third Army has always attacked, and therefore better than 70 percent of our tank casualties have occurred from dug-in antitank guns and not enemy tanks, whereas a majority of the enemy tanks put out have been put out by our tanks.

"'In the current operation, had the 4th Armored Division been equipped with Tiger and Panther tanks and been required to make the move from Saarguemines to Arlon, then through to Bastogne, from Bastogne to the Rhine, and now to Mainz, it would have been necessary to re-armor it twice; and furthermore, it would have had serious if not insurmountable difficulty in crossing rivers.

"'Finally, we must remember that all our tanks have to be transported on steamers and the difference between 40 tons and 70 tons is very marked. The 70-ton tank could never have been brought ashore in landing boats as many of our medium tanks were. Nor could they have marched from the Cotentin Peninsula to the Rhine as practically all of our tanks have been required to do.

"'In mechanical endurance and ease of maintenance, our tanks are infinitely superior to any tank in the theater of war. The outstanding advantage which our tanks possess over the German tank is the mechanical traverse and stabilizer, through the use of which we get most of our kills.'"

Not all Army generals agreed with Patton's comments. Brig. Gen. J. H. Collier, commanding Combat Command A of the 2nd AD, stated in a report to Gen. Dwight D. Eisenhower, March 20, 1945:

"It is my opinion that press reports of statements by high ranking officers to the effect that we have the best equipment in the world do much to discourage the soldier who is using equipment that he knows to be inferior to that of the enemy.

"The fact that our equipment must be shipped over long distances does not, in the opinion of our tankers, justify our inferiority. The M4 has proven inferior to the German Mark VI in Africa before the invasion of Sicily, 10 July 1943."

While Patton's confidence in the Sherman may have been justified when looking at the overall picture of combat in Europe, for the typical Sherman crewman it was a much different view. Knowing that German tanks and antitank weapons, hiding in defensive positions, would probably get the first shot in, Sherman tankers had little desire to be the lead tank on any combat operation. They knew that the thin armor on their vehicles offered little or no protection from the enemy's weapons.

The following narrative from the files of the 5th AD describes what it was like to ride in the first Sherman in a large column spearheading into Germany in 1945. One of the division's veterans, 1st Lt. Marvin W. Orgill of Caliente, Nevada, a 200lb tanker, winner of the Bronze Star in France and the Silver Star in Germany, relates the nerve-wracking feelings.

"As long as you are in the seventh or eighth tank, you feel good. Everything's fine, you feel as safe as in a church. But then the Colonel gets on the radio and says to you, 'Move up to the point of the column.' Then everything changes.

"You move up and the leading tankers wave as you pass and you grin back, but you feel like a fake because you don't feel like grinning. You get up there and the radio comes on and the Battalion Commander wants to know what the hell is holding up the column.

So does the Combat Commander and the Company Commander. You say to yourself, 'Why don't those guys relax?' You say over the radio, 'My platoon is moving out.'

"Behind you, four other tanks cruise fifty yards apart. You watch every bush, tree, house and hole in front. You call over the interphone (intercom) and tell the driver to kick it up to 15 miles per hour. The radio squawks and the Battalion Commander comes in. He wants to know what's holding up the column. You call him back and say, 'Dammit, nothing is holding up the column; you're moving 15 miles per hour.' He calls back and wants to know why you can't make it 20. You bang the microphone back on the hook and don't answer.

"You begin to get that tingling feeling in the back of your neck. There's no good reason for it, but you get it, and whenever you feel it, you usually run into trouble. You tell your gunner to spatter the patch of wood ahead and he does it with his machine gun. Other tanks join in. Then from the woods comes a spurt of flame. If you're lucky the shell misses. You talk your gunner into the target and in five seconds he fires the 75mm.

"He fires again and his second shot is on the target. Three more rounds go out fast. Your platoon has deployed to the right and left and all are firing now. Suddenly there is an explosion in the woods and a German vehicle ahead begins to burn. Two more explosions and two more fires. Your stomach begins to uncurl. All the tanks are firing. They shoot up everything in front and nothing shoots back. For the first time you notice that you are sweating and trembling. You don't say anything, but you reach down and give a pat on the shoulder to your Corporal gunner. He turns around and grins.

Having driven off the road into a muddy ditch, this M4E5 Sherman, armed with a 105mm howitzer, shows a new front hull (designed in 1943) that did away with the protruding hatch hoods found on earlier welded-hull Sherman tanks. The new, larger driver and assistant driver hatches are also shown. *US Army*

Lt. John B. Roller with the American Army in Europe displays a captured German Panzerfaust 60mm antitank weapon. This German bazooka-type weapon comes in two sections: the firing tube with sights and the grenade. When fired, the grenade is stabilized by fins which flare out at the tail. The tube is discarded after firing. *US Army*

"The Battalion Commander comes up to your tank in a peep (jeep). He wants to know what in the hell is holding up the column. You point to the three burning vehicles and he takes a look through his binoculars. Then he climbs up on the turret, map in hand, and you can see he looks as tired as you feel. He unfolds his map and points his finger to a town 15 miles away. He tells you he wants to be there by noon. Then he jumps off the tank.

"You just nod and tell your driver to move out. The burning vehicles are forgotten. You are worried about the next corner and the patch of woods after that and the solitary farmhouse after that. Your stomach begins to curl as you approach the bend in the road. Someone is on the radio, but you don't catch who it is. He wants to know, 'What's holding up the column?'"

Japanese Antitank Weapons

On the other side of the world, the Sherman saw action with British forces in the Far East and with American forces in the Pacific island-hopping campaign.

The threat to the Sherman was far different when facing the Japanese military than when facing the German Army with its Tiger tanks and 88mm antitank guns. From the book *Tanks Are Mighty Fine Things*, a British Sherman tanker in Burma wrote:

"In a recent action, a Jap officer climbed on the back of a tank (Sherman)

Two American soldiers in Europe demonstrate a captured German Army Panzerschreck rocket launcher. Similar in appearance and operation to the American bazooka, the German weapon was a larger caliber and packed a more powerful punch. *US Army*

An American soldier of the 2nd AD examines damage done to the front of an M4A1 Sherman tank by a German Army Panzerfaust during a test on March 14, 1945. The cement bags added to the front of the vehicle for extra protection were blown away from the point of impact. The enemy round passed clear through the transmission armor casting into the vehicle's lower hull.
US Army

and struck the tank commander with his sword, killing him instantly. He then entered the tank and killed the gunner with his sword. The wireless operator (radioman/loader) fired his revolver but managed only to wound the Jap. The two fell to the floor of the turret in hand-to-hand combat. The wireless operator managed to grab the revolver of the dead gunner and finally killed the enemy officer."

While the above method of antitank warfare by the Japanese Army was somewhat rare, the individual bravery of Japanese soldiers and their willingness to sacrifice themselves in an attempt to destroy an M4 are well documented. The Japanese Army fielded few tanks in the numerous island assaults conducted by American military forces in the Pacific or the British military campaign to retake Burma. As a result, the Japanese forces confronting the Sherman depended mostly on antitank guns and close-in attacks by Japanese infantrymen carrying grenades or hollow-charge and magnetic mines.

This is not to say that the Japanese Army had few tanks. At the beginning of the war, the Japanese tank inventory was the fourth largest in the world, following those of the Soviet Union, France, and Germany. But most of its tanks were stationed in China throughout the war. What tanks it did use in operations against American military forces tended to be inferior in both firepower and armor

Racing by a destroyed German 88mm antiaircraft gun, a Sherman tank has its front hull covered with sandbags. Added for extra protection, the sandbags sometimes pre-detonated the warheads of antitank weapons. This was not always the case, but it worked often enough for many tank crews to create very elaborate methods for attaching a large number of sandbags to their vehicles.
US Army

protection, when compared to the Sherman.

The main Japanese antitank gun was the Type 1 47mm. It had a muzzle velocity of 2,735fps and was capable of pene-

trating 2in of steel tank armor at 300yd. This gun was responsible for about one-third of the damaged or destroyed American tanks in the theater. This gun was the same as the one mounted in the Japanese Type 97 Shinhoto Chi-Ha tank.

Other Japanese Army antitank weapons included the Type 94 37mm antitank gun and the Type 97 20mm antitank rifle with a seven-round magazine and automatic feed. Neither of these weapons firing solid shot round proved effective against the Sherman.

For close-range attacks, the Japanese Army had both hand-thrown grenades and a 40mm rifle grenade that could be

fired from the standard Japanese 6.5mm or 7.7mm rifles.

The most deadly weapon the Japanese had for destroying the Sherman was specially-trained tank-hunting infantry units. These soldiers were experts in infiltrating American lines and attacking Shermans parked for the night. They also ambushed individual tanks or tanks that had outrun their infantry support. Favorite spots for attacks were river crossing points and crossroads where Shermans were bunched up and channeled through one small area. Command tanks were a prime target for these units. Japanese soldiers could easily spot command tanks be-

To prevent Japanese soldiers from placing magnetic mines on their tank, this Marine Corps crew attached wooden planking to the sides of their vehicle's hull and suspension system. To stop Japanese soldiers from climbing on their vehicle and placing satchel charges on the thinner armor of the hatches, these Marines welded large nails to the top surface on the turret and front hull around the driver and assistant-driver hatches.
US Marine Corps

cause they had an extra hull-mounted radio antenna. The Japanese tank-hunting parties employed snipers to pick off any tank commander who put his head out of his turret.

Typical Japanese tank-hunting tactics involved two-man teams. One soldier threw a mine under the tank's tracks while the second soldier diverted the tank crew's attention by throwing grenades on top of the vehicle's engine deck.

Another method involved something called a lunge mine. It consisted of a large hollow-charge mine warhead fitted on the end of a 6ft pole. When an M4 was close, the Japanese soldier stood up, rushed the tank, and lunged at its side as if making a bayonet attack, hoping the resulting explosion would destroy the tank. On the minus side, the explosion also destroyed the attacker. For the Japanese soldier, being killed was a small price to pay since he was doing it for the Emperor, his country, and the honor of his unit.

Japanese soldiers also used satchel charges (nothing more than a pack full of high explosives). They ran up to an M4 placed the charges on top of the tank's hatches (normally made of thinner armor than the rest of the tank), and set them off. In response, the Sherman tankers welded nails or steel grating over their hatches to provide some sort of stand-off protection to dissipate the resulting blast. To protect the thin armor on the rear decks of the Sherman engine compartment from both satchel charges or magnetic mines, Sherman crews covered the entire area with a thick layer of sandbags.

To provide additional stand-off protection from Japanese magnetic mines, Sherman crews attached a variety of non-magnetic items, such as wooden planks, to the sides of their vehicles. Other methods included mixing wet paint with sand and applying it to the vehicle. Some crews went so far as to attach a layer of ready-mix concrete to the sides of their vehicles. German late-war tanks on the

Being reloaded with 75mm main gun ammo, this platoon of Marine Corps M4A3 Sherman tanks shows how some vehicles were fitted with steel grating over the crew's hatches. On the rear deck of these vehicles is a layer of sandbags for additional protection. *US Marine Corps*

Russian front had faced a similar magnetic mine threat from Soviet infantry and had been covered with a concrete paste to deflect the mines. British Shermans in Burma were fitted with wire netting over the entire hull and engine deck area to protect against magnetic mines or sticky charges being attached to the tank by individual Japanese soldiers.

Japanese soldiers did not always hand-carry their antitank mines into combat. Combined with tank traps (large trenches), Japanese minefields could be most effective against Shermans. From a 1949 US Army manual on land-mine warfare comes the following.

"The Japanese lacked sound tactical policies in the employment of mines and booby traps. Individual Japanese field commanders were allowed to decide the policy for the employment of mines; hence, wide variances in tactics and doc-

trine. However, certain tactics are standardized by logical reasoning and are similar in all armies.

"Captured Japanese notes state that mines are to be used in front of defensive positions, in dead spaces, and near wire entanglements, and that they are to be installed about 3 to 5 yards apart. The Japanese also employed mines in defiled areas which could not be covered by direct small-arms fire.

"At the start of World War II, the Japanese had only a few types of mines and as they were on the offensive and the use of mines was not emphasized, their mine development fell behind. Later, when forced on the defensive, they discovered that mines were a good defensive weapon. Thus, new and more effective types of mines came into existence. In the defense of Saipan, they employed several new mines, as well as improvised land mines and naval mines.

"The Japanese displayed ingenuity in choosing sites for their mines. Occasionally, they sent patrols inside our lines at night to install mines. The Japanese installed mines under wooden ramps leading up to trestle bridges under edges of bamboo corduroying at fords; in all roads suitable for tank use; in the shoulders of roads, sometimes far enough to the side

to escape detectors and yet near enough to catch a vehicle which might try to pass another; and in dry paddy fields which might be used as tank parks.

"In the latter stages of the Saipan operations when the Japanese knew that no reinforcements were coming, they started a delaying action. Although their supply, communication, and transportation systems were disorganized and they could not lay mines systematically, the Japanese used mines they had on hand and improvised several variations. Two patterns noted in the laying of 63-kilogram aerial bombs, installed at an angle of about 45 degrees to the direction of enemy approach."

New Types of Protection

Because of the heavy toll of Shermans being destroyed by both Japanese and German hollow-charge weapons, the US Army began a number of development programs aimed at fielding both passive and reactive types of protection systems.

Since the weight-carrying capacity of the Sherman design prevented the addition of more steel armor, the United States developed a plastic armor kit that could be fitted to the vehicle's hull and turret. The armor consisted of plastic plates about 10in thick attached by steel cables to brackets welded to the tank. The plastic armor could stop a German Panzerfaust or Panzerschreck round, but the steel cables proved to be vulnerable to attack by high-explosive (HE) rounds.

Another experimental method of defeating hollow-charged weapons involved covering the tank with large metal spikes (about 7–8in long). The theory was that hollow-charge projectiles would break up on the spikes before going off properly. This development program never went into production.

The Army also tested a number of self-protection systems. One system involved mounting a small flame-thrower on all four corners of the tank. The four projectors could be fired separately or all together. Other ideas toyed with included mounting everything from hand grenades and attaching antipersonnel mines and explosive loaded pipe sections along both sides of the hull and turret. Because of the danger of accidental activation in combat and, consequently, the danger to friendly troops, the US Army rejected all these defensive methods.

Chapter 3

Mobility

When France fell to the Germans, American military leaders were convinced that highly mobile operations could defeat an army unable or unwilling to move. German tanks, which French and British tanks generally outgunned during the 1941 invasion of France, showed that firepower alone was no match against a lesser degree of firepower coupled with mobility. For this reason, American military leaders in the early stages of World War II decided that a war of movement was the only sure way to defeat an enemy, and they designed their new Sherman tank for mobility—even at the expense of firepower and armor protection.

Engines

Because of the lack of money between wars, no company had developed a plan to build a dedicated tank engine in the United States. As a result, the US Army was forced to use aircraft engines at the beginning of the war. The following information on the development of the

The M4A3 had the cast differential and final-drive housing. With its 1100ci Ford GAA V-8 of 500hp, the M4A3 was the most popular Sherman among American tankers. *Michael Green*

The M2 light tank series vehicles were the first US Army tanks to feature an aircraft-type, air-cooled, radial engine. In this picture, two Army tank mechanics have removed the rear engine deck of this M2A3 light tank as they try to repair the radial engine that powers this vehicle. The M2A3 light tank had two twin one-man turrets both armed with a single machine gun. This vehicle never saw combat during World War II. *US Army*

Wright R-975 engine is based on World War II Ordnance records found in the National Records Center located in Suitland, Maryland.

Wright R-975

The engine chosen was a 9cyl Wright Whirlwind aircraft engine known as the R-975 and rated at 400hp. This radial air-cooled engine was not a new design. In fact, as an aircraft engine used in training planes and other light planes, improved types were gradually replacing the R-975 engine at the time.

Adaptation of the aircraft engine for use in tanks required a number of modifications. To obtain the highly variable speeds required in tank operation, the engineers changed the intake and exhaust cams to decrease the valve overlap, obtain higher torque at low rpm, and improve idling characteristics. Engineers also modified the magnetos for full automatic spark advance instead of the manual control used in aircraft. The carburetor intake system was redesigned to accommodate oil-bath air cleaners. The front end of the crankshaft was shortened 3/4in to allow for the clutch and flywheel as-

When the M3 medium tank was being designed and built, the US Army naturally decided to fit the radial engine that they had liked so much in the M2/M2A1 medium tanks into the M3. Pictured during the November 1941 South Carolina maneuvers is an M3 medium tank of the famous 2nd AD. The two tank crew members wear the pre-war doughnut-shaped brown leather tanker's crash helmet. *US Army*

sembly. In addition, the front crankcase section was modified to provide for the extra support needed for the flywheel clutch and cooling fan, which were all carried by the crankshaft. Because the engine was mounted at an angle of 10deg from the vertical inside the Sherman's engine compartment, a new carburetor elbow was designed to allow the carburetor to remain vertical.

Early use of the R-975 in the M2 and M2A1 medium tanks resulted in certain changes in the engine and its installation. An auxiliary sump was added to assist in collecting the oil in the two bottom cylinders, and an oil line was provided from which oil could be drained, excessive amounts of which caused sluggish action of the governor. The length of various ignition harness components was reduced, and a dust protection bonnet was installed over the accelerator-pump mechanism, which had a tendency to become fouled. The danger of hydrostatic lock, always a troublesome feature of radial engines, was reduced with a quick cutoff device that prevented drainage of fuel from the carburetor after the driver had shut off the ignition and while the vehicle coasted to a stop.

To reduce the hazard from fire, the outlet for the engine cooling air was moved from the rear of the top deck to the upper part of the rear plate. (The opening was now protected by an exten-

sion of the top deck.) This arrangement, however, exhausted the cooling air counter to the exhaust. The resulting turbulence created an appreciable loss in power.

Nevertheless, the R-975 engine thus modified proved satisfactory in the M2 and M2A1 medium tanks. On August 26, 1940, the American Tank Committee met at Aberdeen, Maryland, to determine the characteristics of the new M3 medium tank. A test was conducted using existing light and medium tanks, which were put through their paces before a number of British tank experts, who were greatly impressed. A British medium tank, which participated in the demonstration, was sluggish in comparison to the American medium tanks.

Naturally then, the same engine appeared in the M3 medium tank. But the M3 weighed over 30 tons fully loaded; the Army found that the tank was underpowered. This was also the experience of the Army during their large-scale Carolina and Louisiana maneuvers in 1941. During the maneuvers, tank crews found that the engine developed as little as 280hp, net. The crews also complained of short engine life because many of the engines lasted fewer than 100hr before a general overhaul was necessary.

The deficient power and short engine life were interrelated and both were the result of difficulties in cooling, unsatisfactory air cleaner and muffler installation, and the high temperature of carburetor air. The high temperature reduces the density of the fuel-air mixture entering the cylinders, reducing their power output. In the lighter M2 medium tanks, the reduction in power was not serious, but in the M3 medium tank it was.

As a result of an extensive series of tests, many proposed remedies for these difficulties followed. The tests began in March 1941 when the first M3 arrived at Aberdeen Proving Ground and extended into 1942.

With the adoption of the M3 and the great expansion in tank production that followed, the manufacture of the R-975 engine was transferred from the Wright Corp. to Continental Motors, and the engine thereafter was known as the Continental R-975-EC2. Wright turned out a total of only 750 engines; by January 1942, Continental's production schedules called for 1,000 a month.

This change in manufacturers caused certain problems because Continental discovered that some of the Wright production drawings were out of date and specified tolerances that caused undue wear and oil consumption. This situation was quickly corrected, but excessive oil consumption (as high as 1gal per hour) continued in spite of the improved engine cooling.

On September 11, 1941, when standardization of the Sherman tank series was recommended, and early in 1942 when production began. The Ordnance Committee's recommendation did not specify the engine, because of the impending adoption of alternate engines. The recommendation merely stated that the powerplant should be able to propel the tank at 25mph on level paved roads and at 12 mph on a 10 percent grade, start at 20deg F, and have satisfactory cooling at 125deg F at sea level. The committee also stated that all gasoline

The M4 Sherman tank series was approved for production on September 11, 1941. Production began in early 1942. Both the M4 welded-hull and M4A1 cast-hull Shermans were built with the Continental

R975 radial engines. This line drawing from an M4 Sherman manual shows the rear hull placement of the engine. Also pictured on either side of the engine access doors are the round pattern air cleaners.

engines must operate on fuels approved by the War Department, which meant 80 octane gasoline. The R-975 was the only tank engine still requiring the aviation fuel.

Some delay occurred in making this change because of uncertainty concerning the most satisfactory compression ratio. At first a 5.2:1 ratio was attempted, then 5.5:1. Both of these seriously decreased the power output, and although it was thought in advance the 5.7:1 would be too high, it turned out to be satisfactory when an engine with that ratio was completed and tested with 80 octane gasoline in April 1942. That month, the project was reported to be complete, and production of the new engine, designated

the R-975-EC2, began on May 11.

Even before production of the R-975-EC2 began, an extensive new program for improving its torque characteristics had been started. A typical complaint against all R-975 models was that the maximum torque was delivered at too high a speed. Diesel engines had just the opposite problem; their highest torque came at low speed. When the R-975 ran into hard pulling, the driver had to shift gears more frequently than with other engines. And if the driver gave the engine full throttle at low speed, the temperature climbed dangerously.

As experimentation continued to improve the R-975, a complete redesign took shape. As a result, the Subcommittee

Pictured on the production line at Lima Locomotive Works are early cast-hull M4A1 tanks powered by the radial R975 engine. Visible are the armored air inlet cover, which the workman stands on, and the large single-piece engine compartment top plate behind the armored air inlet cover. Directly at the rear of the engine compartment are two fully exposed dual rear engine access doors.
US Army

on Automotive Equipment recommended R-975-C4, a new designation, on April 30, 1943. The committee stated that the new engine increased the gross torque and the gross horsepower, while increasing fuel economy by 10 percent.

The recommendation to procure 2,000 of the new engines was approved on June 17, 1943, with the provision that they be used only on the M18 Hellcat Tank Destroyer. Evidently the engine was such a great improvement that by the following October the British requested it be installed in all medium tanks supplied to them that used the R-975. In February 1944, the Armored Force Board, following tests of the R-975-C4 in M4A1s, requested that it replace the original R-975 engine in the earlier Shermans. These tests revealed a 35 percent increase in oil economy, a 10 percent increase in power, a decrease of 50deg in cylinder head temperatures, and superior piston ring and overall engine life. The request included the statement that the R-975-C4 should be used "exclusively in supplementing the Ford tank engine, model GAA, in meeting Medium Tank requirements for US troops." With the approval of this recommendation on April 13, 1944, the original R-975, which had been the principal medium tank engine

for nearly six years, became a substitute.

The R-975 was used in a greater number of different types of vehicles than any other engine in its class. In spite of numerous shortcomings, the great number of R-975 engines used by the American, British, Canadian, French, and Russian forces can be said to have contributed as much as any other single mechanism to the winning of the war.

GM Twin Diesel

A GM twin diesel engine powered the M4A2. The engines, two 6cyl, 2-stroke, liquid-cooled diesel truck engines, had a total rated output of 375hp and a displacement of 850ci. The two engines, each of which could operate independently, were mounted alongside each other and joined by a heavy junction plate at their fan ends and a double-clutch housing and transfer case at the flywheel ends. The radiators were located at the rear of the engine compartment.

Power from each engine was transmitted through the vehicle's clutch to its transfer unit, which in turn transmits the power to the propeller shaft. In normal operations, a single clutch pedal controlled the two clutches, but a control on the hand throttle bracket could lock out either clutch. If necessary, the M4A2 tank

driver could use only one engine.

The twin GM diesel engines fitted to the M4A2 tank gave it an excellent horse-power-to-weight ratio. The diesel engine's high torque characteristics provided the vehicle with much better cross-country performance and cruising range than the gasoline-engine-powered M4 and M4A1 tanks. On the down side, the M4A2 diesel engines were more sensitive to dirt in the intake air.

The U. S. Army Desert Warfare Board, after testing 12 M4A2s, reported that when the tank was in first class mechanical condition, it had an excellent horsepower-to-weight ratio, the ability to sustain 30mph on dirt roads, and good cross-country speed and lugging ability. The board criticized the air cleaners, cooling system, and clutches. It concluded that the M4A2, as originally delivered by the manufacturer, was not a satisfactory combat vehicle owing to the faulty design of the powerplant and attendant mechanical weaknesses. The board also stated that the suspension system was not adequate for the additional weight imposed on it by the engine and recommended that tests be continued on the modified M4A2.

In February 1943, six improved M4A2s were shipped to the Desert Warfare Board in Southern California for additional tests. Five of these vehicles had improved engine installations, including larger air cleaners, improved cooling, a single throttle control, heavier clutch springs, semi-metallic clutch facings, and a clutch-equalizer linkage. The sixth vehicle had all of the above improvements and an improved engine lubrication system, which eliminated the oil tank and incorporated a wet sump in each of the engines.

In May 1943, after conducting a continuous endurance test of ten improved M4A2s with an equal number of M4, M4A3, and M4A4 tanks, the Armored

This beautifully restored M4A3 belongs to a private collector in the midwest. This tank has appeared in several movies and television commercials. *Michael Green*

Force Board reported that the performance of the GM twin-engine units was substantially equal to that of the best engine in the test. The earliest failure occurred at 75hr. Two GM engine units (comprised of two engine each) completed the test at 400hr. The fuel and oil economy were considered satisfactory for this type of engine. The number of man-hours of engine maintenance required was second best of the four engines tested. The clutches on these engines were improved over previous ones. The engine's main weakness was its sensitivity to dirt. A need for improving the air cleaner was noted.

The twin-diesel engine set-up was later tested at Aberdeen Proving Ground from October 1943 to February 1944 in competition again with other standard engines. From this test, the Aberdeen Proving Grounds and the Ordnance Branch concluded that the endurance qualities of twin-diesel engine units were unpredictable and that their reliability was the lowest of the group. Fuel consumption was also lower than that of the gasoline engines but was higher than that of the Caterpillar diesel in the M4A6 Sherman. Oil consumption was lower than for the other engines. Maintenance requirements were satisfactory, but were considered excessive when clutch maintenance was included.

In accordance with a War Department order issued in March 1942, diesel-powered tanks were not sent overseas with US troops. This decision was made because of the greater availability of gasoline. At the time, all US military wheeled and tracked vehicles were gasoline powered. Of the 8,053 M4A2 tanks produced during the war in American factories, most were shipped overseas to the Soviet Union and England. Some M4A2 tanks saw training duties in the US, and a few saw action in North Africa with the 1st AD. The US Marine Corps also employed M4A2 tanks during their Pacific island-hopping campaigns.

Diesel-engine tanks saw widespread use with Soviet and Japanese armored units. The German Army used gasoline-powered tank engines throughout the war. Most American tankers who fought in gasoline-powered Shermans believed that their vehicles were more prone to catching fire when hit by enemy weapons than a diesel-powered vehicle. In actual practice, most gasoline-powered Shermans caught fire because of hits in the ammunition stowage areas.

Sherman tank crews tended to make this problem worse by carrying as many as 30–40 extra 75mm main gun tank rounds inside their vehicles. Human nature being what it is, it's understandable

This M4A3 Sherman is equipped with the early VVSS system. *Michael Green*

The US Army didn't think much of the M4A4 Sherman with the Chrysler A57 multibank engine. As a result, most of them were supplied under Lend-Lease to the British and Commonwealth armies. Pictured is a Canadian Army M4A4 tank during World War II parked next to a damaged church in Holland. *Canadian Army*

that crews felt safer when they did not have to depend on ammunition trucks that may or may not reach them in time. But with the Sherman's thin armor protection, any penetration by an enemy antitank weapon would normally set off an onboard ammunition propellant fire and burn out the tank.

Ford GAA V–8

As the demand for aircraft engines dried up supplies of the R-975 radial engines (as fitted in the M4 and M4A1 Sher-

mans), the Army looked for other options. In late 1941, Ford Motor Co. developed a liquid-cooled V–8 gasoline-powered engine known as the model GAA.

Based on an experimental Ford V–12 aircraft engine that never went into production, Ford's new engine developed 500hp with an engine displacement of 1100ci, a big improvement over the R-975's 400hp.

Because of its high output, compactness, and excellent power-to-weight ratio, in January 1942 the US Army authorized the Ford engine for use in the Sherman and designated the new model as the M4A3.

The GAA engine featured a number of innovative design features including the extensive use of aluminum castings to save weight. The GAA engine could be broken down into five major subassemblies; that was its most important feature.

Each of these subassemblies comprised an integral unit for easy handling and replacement. In contrast, the R-975 radial engine on the M4 and M4A1 Sherman models was so laid out that even the replacement of minor components could require the removal of the entire engine from the vehicle.

The Ford GAA engine as fitted to the M4A3 tank drove the vehicle through the same powertrain as earlier model Shermans.

The accessory drive was a unit many considered one of the most interesting subassemblies of the engine. This unit was a small package consisting of an aluminum bracket supporting enough gears to provide for seven individual takeoffs. The seven included the hourglass worm gear driving the two camshaft drives, one for each bank; the three bevel gears providing the two fan drives, one for each

Because the M4A4 Sherman was longer than other Sherman tank models, Chrysler was forced to install longer tracks and lengthen the spaces between the vehicle's bogie wheels. This particular M4A4 Sherman is in Burma in February, 1945. Operated by an American crew, the vehicle is being used to support Chinese troops fighting the Japanese Army. *US Army*

side of the engine; the magneto drive pinion; the water pump drive; and the oil pump drive.

This assembly was bolted to the cam drive end of the crankcase driven by a quill shaft splined into the crankshaft. This quill shaft functioned as a cushion against torsional vibrations of the crankshaft that would normally be transmitted to the gear unit. In addition, the quill shaft also functioned as a fuse, if the loads imposed on the assembly exceeded

the design limitations of 90hp. The aluminum casting and cover supported the two magnetos and the magneto drive water pump assembly.

The oil pan, which was also an aluminum casting, was ultimately designed in two compartments carrying the oil-intake screens and pipes with a double pump that was driven by a quill from the previously mentioned accessory drive, thus enabling removal of this assembly without disturbing any other part of the engine.

Not only was the engine designed in separate assemblies, but it also was designed to operate on either or both banks of cylinders. This was made possible by using a separate 4cyl magneto for each bank of cylinders.

The spark-plug wires were carried to the camshaft covers via titeflex conduit. The camshaft cover, also an aluminum casting, was so designed that along with

covering and sealing the camshafts, a trough between the two camshafts provided space for the spark-plug wires as well as making the spark plugs accessible for maintenance and replacement. This trough was covered by a thin sheet metal plate, thus protecting the wires from damage, shielding them against radio interference, and giving the engine a clean smooth appearance.

The GAA engine was the preferred engine by most tankers. If sufficient production capacity had existed at the time, the Army would have chosen to fit all of its various Sherman models with the Ford GAA engine.

Comparing the Radial to the Ford Engine

Skip Warvel, curator of the Indiana Military Museum, Inc., which has the largest collection of Shermans in the United States, compares the Sherman ra-

This old rusted M4A1 Sherman was saved from a Marine Corps firing range. Besides being a rare flame-thrower tank version, this vehicle has extended end connectors (nicknamed duckbills) fitted on both sides of the tracks, giving it improved mobility over soft ground. The vehicle also features the early-style three-piece steel casting that formed the differential and final drive casing. *Michael Green*

dial engine to the Ford engine.

"The radial engine, compared to the Ford engine, is bigger and takes up more space. Being air-cooled, it needs to have air come in, and needs to have that air out in a fairly constant flow. You need your seals in place so the air flows the right way. If you forget to put a couple of seals in when you're restoring your tank, your engine is going to overheat and

you'll probably never quite know why.

Radial engines are a little more temperamental, being an air-cooled engine. They also run hotter than a water-cooled engine so the parts, when they're cold, say ambient temperature of 70deg, have more space between them because as they get hot, they need more room to grow, so when they're at running temperature they fit correctly. A liquid-cooled

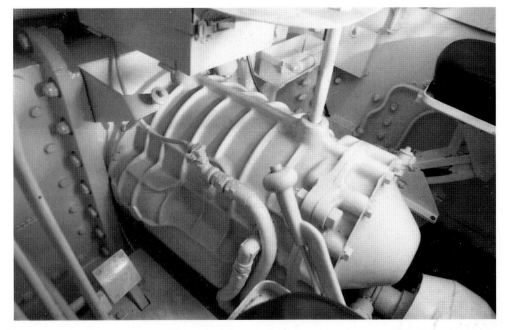

Pictured inside an M4A1 Sherman hull is the vehicle's transmission. The unit generated a lot of heat when in prolonged operation.

That heat made the driver's and assistant driver's positions very uncomfortable. *Michael Green*

engine like the Ford doesn't run quite so hot and also doesn't need as much space to grow so they're just a little easier to get started. That's not to say that the radial is hard to get started, if you've got a good rebuilt engine, it will start right up and be very reliable.

"From the driving standpoint, the radial engine was really designed for an airplane and is more of a constant speed type of engine. With a tank, its just the opposite, you've got a five-speed manual transmission, and when you accelerate, you've got to shift through the gears. If you wind the engine all the way to redline, which I believe on the R-975 engine is 2850rpm, then you shift from second to third gear—normally you wouldn't start it in first, that's just a creeper gear, a pulling gear—you're going to go from 2850 down to 2000 or maybe 1800rpm. The engine really doesn't have that much power at that point. It's a 450hp engine but at that point you've only got 200hp. It's not until you get to a certain rpm that you attain your maximum horsepower and your maximum torque.

"With a Ford V8, you can put it in second gear and start at idle speed, no problem. If you try that in a radial, nine times out of ten, you'll kill it. It just doesn't have the power to move 62,500lb forward at idle. So from a driving standpoint, it's much easier to drive the Ford engine than the radial engine.

"In driving a Sherman's manual transmission, momentum is the key. On the later tanks, which were automatic, the momentum helps, but you don't have to shift. Your transmission shifts for you and so you don't have to worry about

slowing down in between shifts. In the Sherman, you may be going through some mud or dirt where there's a lot of resistance to your forward motion, so you accelerate to full throttle in second gear. By the time you've pushed in the clutch, shifted the old nonsynchro transmission (well some of the gears are synchro but 3rd, 4th and 5th aren't), shifted into third gear, you could almost come to a complete stop and you almost have to go back over and start again. So having an engine with a lot of power throughout its rpm range just makes it much easier to drive. You can slow down and clank the thing into third at 1000rpm and still accelerate along and do it much quicker in a Ford Sherman tank than you can in the radial Sherman tank."

Chrysler A57 Multibank

Unfortunately, the Army was still short of the required number of tank engines needed for all the Shermans coming off the assembly lines. Since it normally takes two years to develop a heavy-duty engine, the only possible quick solution was to use multiple existing automobile engines. Chrysler decided to combine five of its 6cyl car engines and connect them to a common crankshaft.

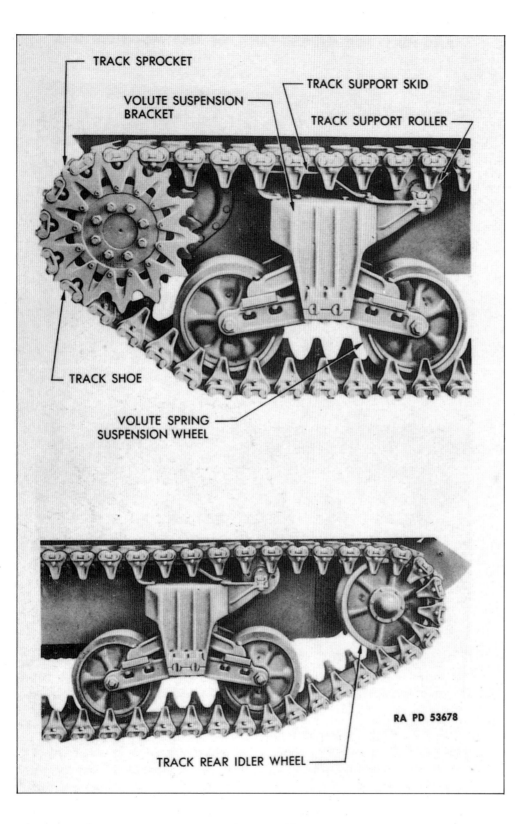

TRACK SPROCKET

VOLUTE SUSPENSION BRACKET

TRACK SUPPORT SKID

TRACK SUPPORT ROLLER

TRACK SHOE

VOLUTE SPRING SUSPENSION WHEEL

TRACK REAR IDLER WHEEL

RA PD 53678

Taken from a US Army manual is this picture showing the various components that make up the early model Vertical Volute Spring Suspension (VVSS) as fitted to all first-generation Sherman tanks. The VVSS system had very little road-wheel travel when com- **pared to German tanks with their more advanced torsion-bar suspension systems. This allowed much heavier German tanks to have superior mobility to the lighter Sherman tank. This fact was always a big surprise to Allied tankers the first time they saw it.**

With a total of 30cyl and five belt-driven water pumps (in the original version), this monstrosity was known as the Chrysler A57 multibank engine. The Sherman's engine compartment had to be lengthened 11in for the engine to fit. Some fuel tanks had to be removed and others enlarged. Blisters were fitted to provide clearance for the cooling fan and the upper parts of the radiator assembly and the filler cap. Because of the engine's extra weight, some suspension system components were relocated for better weight distribution. Longer tracks were needed to accommodate the increased length of the hull. With the multibank engine and an all-welded hull, this model was the M4A4 Sherman.

The US Army felt that the M4A4 Sherman with the Chrysler A57 multibank engine was not a satisfactory unit when compared to other Sherman engines then in production.

The Army's major problem with the multibank engine design was its complexity. Because of its size, many of its engine components were inaccessible for maintenance or repair unless the entire engine was pulled from the vehicle. As a result, the Army gave the great majority of the 7,499 M4A4 Sherman tanks built to the British military under Lend-Lease. In British service the M4A4 Sherman was considered a satisfactory vehicle when its crews were prepared with the proper maintenance training.

Caterpillar D200A

The least-known engine fitted to the Sherman series was the Caterpillar D200A, a modification of a Wright G200 9cyl air-cooled radial engine designed to operate as a diesel with fuel injection. This modified engine was capable of operating on a wide variety of petroleum products ranging from crude oil to high-octane gasoline. It produced 450hp at 2000rpm on 40 cetane diesel oil and had a displacement of 1,823ci. The Sherman with this engine was designated the M4A6. The engine itself was later redesignated as the Ordnance Engine RD1820.

Chrysler had started production of the M4A6 tank in October 1943, but ended production in February 1944 after building only 75 vehicles. The US Army had decided that the M4A6 was not needed since only gasoline-powered Shermans were to serve overseas in US Army tank formations.

On display at a museum in Southern California, this badly shot-up M4 composite hull Sherman came off a US Air Force firing range. The vehicle features the rubber-coated steel tracks found on many Sherman tanks until a rubber shortage forced the Army to switch to all-steel tracks. *Greg Stewart*

Differential, Transmission, and Final Drive

The nose of the Sherman hull is a steel casting that forms the differential and final drive casing. The five-speed synchromesh transmission was attached to the rear of the differential casing and occupied the center of the front hull compartment, to the left of which was located the driver's seat and controls and at the right, a seat for the assistant driver. Synchromesh units on third, fourth, and fifth gears incorporated a locking device that prevented gears engaging until the pinion speeds were synchronized. Three selector rods with locking devices were housed on the right side of the gearbox and connected to the gear lever through a yoke and link which were supported on two pins located at the rear of the gearbox.

The transmission incorporated a pressure-feed lubrication system in which a pump, driven from one of the shafts, forces oil to the output shaft pinion bearings via an oil cooler, which was located in the fighting compartment bulkhead, above the propeller-shaft housing. The speedometer drive was taken from the rear end of the gearbox output shaft and was connected to the housing.

Early Shermans were fitted with a parking brake at the rear of the gearbox casing. The brake consists of two cones, one fixed to the rear of the gearbox output shaft, the other splined to the housing. By operating the lever, the splined cone could be made to slide forward and bind on the output shaft cone, and so hold it stationary. This brake was constructed for the sole purpose of holding the vehicle stationary, and it wasn't to be used for slowing down or stopping. On later models, a different parking device was fitted.

The differential on the Sherman was

Chrysler employees are carefully lowering a very large A57 multibank engine unit into the rear hull of an M4A4 Sherman. Because the engine unit consisted of five car engines mated together, the engine compartment of the M4A4 Sherman had to be lengthened 11in for it to fit. *General Dynamics*

called a controlled-differential because it not only transmitted engine power to the final drive units, but also contained brake drums for the purpose of steering and stopping the tank. With this arrangement both tracks were driven when steering.

A disadvantage of the Sherman's system is that its heavy-duty truck-type differential and non-boosted brakes made it impossible to make a pivot turn (very useful in tank combat) and physically difficult for the driver to make a complete skid turn, unless the terrain he was turning on was very smooth (such as ice). The Sherman's normal minimum turn radius was about 80ft.

Controlled-differential steering was dropped from American tank designs after the war because newer heavy tanks coming into postwar service overloaded the system. Better suited for lighter armored vehicles, the controlled differential steering system was used until recently in the M113 armored personnel carriers.

Most American-built tanks developed after the Sherman used a cross-drive transmission that incorporated a triple differential steering system. This allowed American tanks to pivot turn.

There were many disadvantages of having the Sherman differential, final drive casing, and transmission in the hull's front. It forced the Sherman's designers to make the vehicle taller than they would have liked since they had to allow extra room for the driveshaft to pass under the

vehicle's turret to transfer power to the front-mounted transmission. Front-mounted transmissions and differentials are more vulnerable to antitank mines because most mines go off under the front sections of vehicles.

Unfortunately, the design layout of the Sherman tank was dictated by the vehicle that it was based on, the M3 medium tank. When the M3 was designed, neither the height of a vehicle nor the future threat of antitank mines influenced American armored vehicle designers.

The Sherman's differential, final drive casing, and transmission generated a lot of heat during operation. On the plus side, built-up heat in the transmission could keep its crew warm for at least a couple of hours on even the coldest night. In operation, some Sherman crews used transmission heat to warm up their food, coffee, or tea.

Suspension

In a tank, which must travel at speed over a variety of different terrain, an efficient suspension system is important to the vehicle's long-term durability, accuracy of fire, and crew comfort.

World War I tanks were supported on track rollers mounted rigidly on the vehicle's hull. There was almost no flexibility, resulting in poor riding qualities for the crew. But as the tanks of the time had a maximum speed of only 4–6mph, it was not an important design problem.

By the 1930s, the US Army had developed a number of high-speed light tanks. The hulls of these vehicles were supported by a spring suspension unit mounted on an axle. Two small metal wheels known as bogie wheels were mounted at the ends of the axle. The bogie wheels distributed the weight of the tank along its tracks. The Sherman hull was supported on six bogie suspension assemblies, three on each side. Each bogie assembly consisted of a spring unit attached to and riding on rubber-rimmed steel wheels. The system was called the Vertical Volute Spring Suspension (VVSS) system.

This basic system was adapted to the M3 tank in 1940 and to the Sherman in 1941. In the early Sherman, a track return roller was mounted on top of the bogie carrying bracket. Later Shermans had the track return roller mounted behind the bogie carrying bracket.

When the VVSS system was fitted to the first Shermans, the military was already aware that the system was inadequate for the demands that were being placed on it. While this suspension system worked quite well for light tanks, it was overwhelmed by the increased weight of the new tanks. The result was a very short life span. The rubber tire material tended to separate from the wheels at speeds above 20mph, and the volute springs would deform or crack under hard use. This system was later improved (see Chapter 7).

Tracks

In World War I, tank tracks consisted of heavy continuous articulated bands of steel shoes connected by steel pins. The pin and shoes wore out rapidly and failures due to broken tracks were frequent.

With the advent of higher speed light tanks in the 1930s, the US military developed rubber-coated steel tracks. Unlike all-steel tracks which were noisy and tore up roads, rubber-coated steel tracks cut down on shock and vibration for the tank crews and allowed operation on highways, at high speed, without damage to the roads.

When the Sherman first came off the production line in 1941, the tracks were comprised of 79 steel-and-rubber blocks linked together to form an endless track. The drive sprockets at the front of the Sherman pulled their tracks from the rear of the vehicle and placed them down in front of the advancing tank. Two idlers, mounted on eccentric shafts at the rear of the vehicle provided for adjustment of the track tension. The upper reach of the track, between the rear idler and front sprocket, was supported and guided by three steel rollers mounted on brackets attached to the bogie brackets.

When fitted with extended end connectors (nicknamed duckbills or duck feet), the Sherman tracks, which were 16.5in wide, could be increased to 20 1/8in wide. These extended end connectors could then be connected to grousers giving the Sherman a track width of 32.5in. Some Shermans had their suspension system spaced out from the vehicle's hull, allowing the use of extended end connectors on both sides of the tracks, giving an effective track width of 23 11/16in and permitting the use of 37in grousers.

Because of rubber shortages, the US Army was forced to start using all-steel tracks on the Shermans beginning in 1942. In service, the steel tracks proved to last longer on rocky terrain than the rubber tracks. A number of different manufacturers built these steel tracks.

So what did American tankers think about the Sherman's mobility as compared to German tanks? Lt. Col. Wilson M. Hawkins, commander of the 3rd TB, 67th AR, made the following statement in a wartime report.

"It has been claimed that our tank is the more maneuverable. In recent tests we put a captured German Mark V against all models of our own. The German tank was the faster, both across country and on the highway and would make sharper turns. It was also the better hill climber."

T. Sgt. Willard D. May of the 2nd AD backed up Hawkins' claim in his report.

"I have taken instructions on the Mark V and have found, first, it is easily as maneuverable as the Sherman; second, the flotation exceeds that of the Sherman; third, driving is about the equal to our Sherman; fourth, the stowage is no better than the Sherman's; fifth, the turret traverse and traverse controls are inferior to that of the Sherman."

S/Sgt. Charles A. Carden, a Sherman platoon sergeant, completes the comparison in his report.

"The Mark V and VI in my opinion have more maneuverability and certainly more flotation. I have seen in many cases where the Mark V and VI tanks could maneuver nicely over ground where the M4 would bog down. On one occasion I saw at least 10 Royal Tigers make a counterattack against us over ground that for us was nearly impossible."

Pictured in the storage yard of a private collector is this R975 engine awaiting the day it can be rebuilt and placed back into a Sherman tank. The R975 engine was a 9cyl, air-cooled, gasoline engine based on an aircraft design. The radial engines used to power the M4 and M4A1 Sherman tanks were considered to be rather underpowered when compared to other Sherman engine types. *Michael Green*

Chapter 4

The Crew

All first-generation Shermans had a five-man crew: driver, assistant driver and bow machine gunner, tank commander, gunner, and loader.

Driver and Assistant Driver

The Sherman driver sat at the left side of the vehicle's front hull, alongside the transmission. The assistant driver/bow gunner sat on the right side of the transmission, opposite the driver. He controlled a .30cal machine gun mounted in the right front of the Sherman's hull.

Two hatches in the front hull of the Sherman provided access to either the driver's or assistant driver's positions. On earlier-model Shermans, the hatch covers opened up and out toward the sides of the tank, but the weight of the hatch covers made closing them difficult from inside the tank.

Sergeant A. D. Childres, of the famous 2nd AD (nicknamed the Hell on Wheels Division), models the standard World War II padded tanker's helmet and goggles. Also pictured is the throat microphones and connecting interphone box on his chest. By flicking a switch on the interphone box, Childres could talk over the tank's intercom or radio system. *US Army*

On later models, the hatch covers opened back onto stops against which

Both the Sherman tank driver and assistant driver sat in the vehicle's front hull. Because there was only one set of controls, if the driver needed to be relieved he traded places with the assistant driver. This 1st AD M4A1 crosses the Arno River in Italy on September 1, 1944. The assistant driver's main job was to fire the .30cal machine gun, which can be seen on the vehicle's lower front hull. This particular vehicle is fitted with all-steel tracks. *US Army*

they were locked by spring catches. The springs attached to the hatch covers steadied them as they were closed and exerted a pull on the hatch covers when they were opened.

Both the driver and assistant driver had adjustable seats with detachable backrests. The seats were mounted on pedestals and were adjustable for height as well as backward and forward movement. The driver and assistant driver each had two periscopes: one fixed periscope provided forward vision only; the other on the hatch cover was mounted so that it could be rotated 360deg and tilted to raise or lower the line of vision. Early model production Shermans had direct-vision slots for emergency use by the driver and assistant driver. These slots were later eliminated because the driver's periscope holders prevented easy use of the vision slots making them somewhat useless.

For driving in poor weather conditions with his hatch open, the Sherman driver was provided with a removable folding hood with a safety glass windshield. The windshield had an electric wiper and an electric defroster which could be plugged into one of the electrical accessory outlet sockets. When not in

Seen in this photo is the Sherman driver's removable folding hood with a safety-glass windshield. The windshield was fitted with an electric wiper and defroster. Used in poor weather conditions, the hood was normally stowed on a tray inside the vehicle. *US Army*

use, the hood was folded and stowed on a tray above the gearbox. Most Sherman tankers do not remember using the removable folding hood very often.

Driving the Sherman

Located in the left front hull of the Sherman was the driver's instrument panel. To start most Sherman tanks (except radial-engine vehicles), the driver followed this procedure: 1) turn the fuel switch to ON; 2) turn the battery master switches to ON; 3) check that gear lever is in neutral and brakes are applied; 4) hold the clutch pedal down or lock out the clutches; 5) test operation of the engine emergency shut-down valves; 6) set the hand throttle in idling position; 7) push in starter button and hold it firmly until the engine starts; 8) check the tachometer to make sure the engine is running and oil pressure gauge to ensure the lubrication system is working; 9) set hand throttle to warming-up speed; 10) slowly engage clutches.

The starting procedure for radial-engine Shermans was a bit more complex than simply pushing in the starter button. Jacques Littlefield, a well-known tank collector, describes what it takes to get a Sherman with a radial engine going.

"On any radial-engine vehicle, before you can start it, you have to turn the engine, making sure its magnetos are off. You put a large hand crank in the back and you then have to turn the engine through about three turns. Now to get three turns through the starter, the driver has to turn about 60 or 70 times on a hand crank located at the rear of the tank. This feature proved to be very unpopular with American tankers as one could expect."

The Sherman driver's gearshift lever was located to his right. There were five forward gears and one reverse gear. The driver had to depress a plunger on top of the shift lever before he could move the lever over to the left for engaging first or reverse gear. When changing into a gear,

62

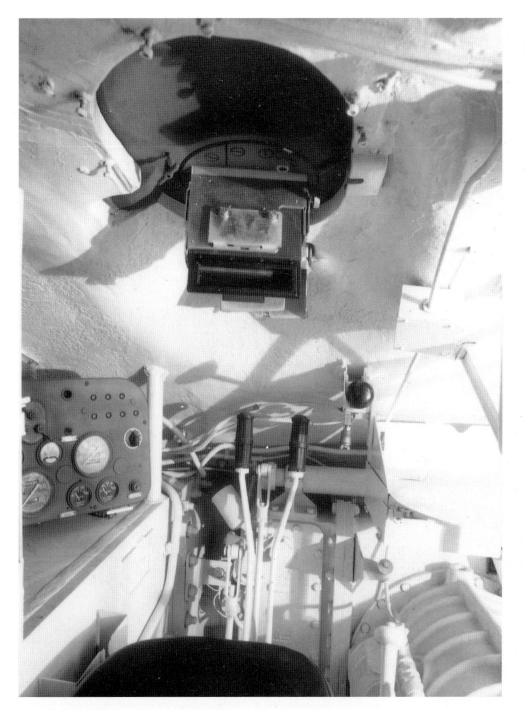

The driver's position inside a cast-hull M4A1 Sherman. On the driver's right is the transmission, on the left is the instrument panel. In the center in front of the driver's seat are the two steering levers. Over the driver's seat is the driver's hatch with its attached periscope. Just visible underneath the hatch-mounted periscope is the mounting frame for the auxiliary periscope, which replaced the direct vision slots found on the first production Shermans. *Michael Green*

the driver moved the shift lever until he felt a resistance. A firm pressure would then be maintained on the shift lever which would then move easily into position.

The Sherman driver was provided with two steering levers mounted on the floor of the vehicle just forward of his seat. The right and left steering levers operated the right and left brakes respectively. The controls were not interconnected;

therefore, operation of one steering lever would have no effect on the opposite brake.

Mounted on the floor directly ahead of the driver's seat and to the right of the steering levers was a foot accelerator pedal. The hand-operated throttle was mounted on the final drive housing and on the right of the steering levers. On the left floor side of the steering levers was a clutch pedal.

With the tank in first gear, the Sherman driver pulled the appropriate steering lever straight back with a smooth, deliberate movement. If he snatched a steering lever, he could put the vehicle into a broadside skid. Turns were done by a series of complete brake applications and not in one partial application which would allow the brake to slip. (The brakes operated in oil and the heat generated by a slipping brake burned the oil on the linings which became glazed and ineffective as a result.)

If the Sherman was moving out in a straight line on level terrain, the driver normally started out in second gear and then shifted through third and fourth, much as you would with an old car. The one thing a Sherman driver never wanted to do was speed up a change or crash a gear by using excessive force on the gear lever. This would result in a serious strain on the vehicle's control linkage and transmission.

To slow down or stop a Sherman, the driver pulled both steering levers back with equal force. Unless the brakes were applied with equal pressure, the tank would steer to one side.

To put the Sherman in reverse, the vehicle had to be at a standstill. With engines idling, the driver held down the clutch pedal, depressed the safety button on the gear shift lever, and moved the lever to the reverse position. In reverse, the speed of the Sherman was not supposed to exceed 3mph with the engine rpm speed not exceeding 1800rpm. To steer in reverse, the Sherman driver worked the steering levers in the same way as when he drove the vehicle forward.

The Sherman took quite a bit of pulling to steer it one way or the other. It was as a result, a very tiring vehicle to steer, especially if you were doing any maneuvering, so the Army tried to select robust soldiers to be tank drivers. Clarence Lancy, who commanded an M4

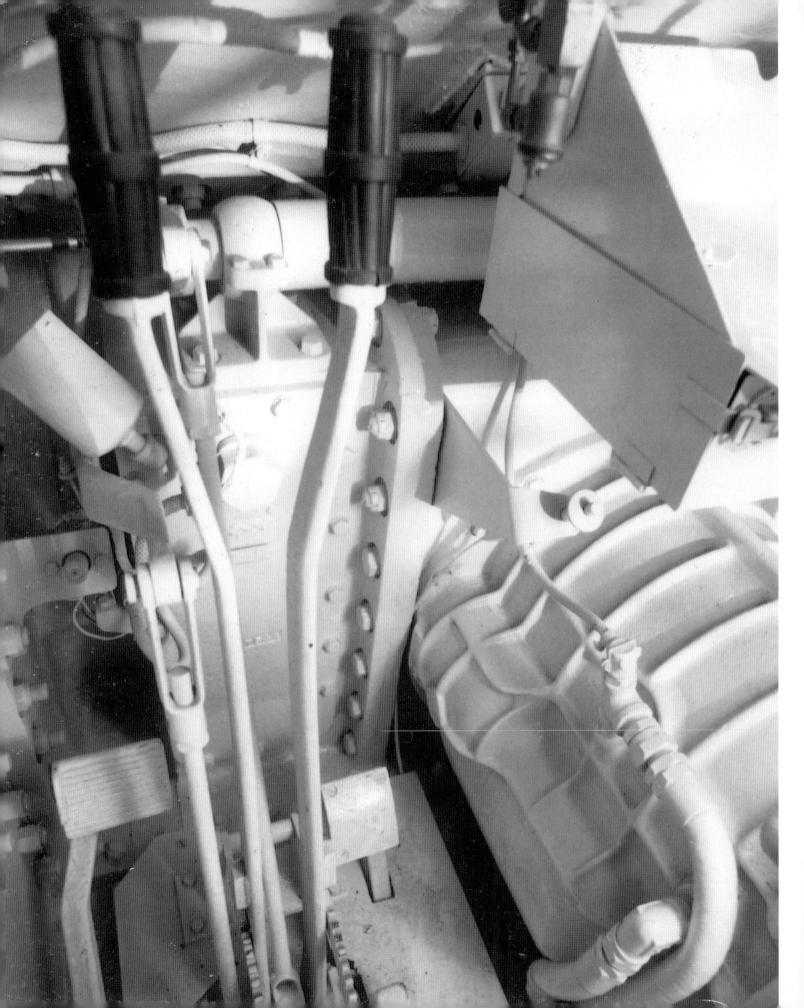

at the US Army's Desert Training Center in Southern California, remembers this selection process:

"We normally picked the biggest guys to be Sherman drivers. It wasn't an easy job. When we got a batch of new trainees, the first thing we did was teach them how to drive our wheeled vehicles. Those who did the best with the trucks usually became tank drivers.

"In general, I remember that most of the tank drivers in our unit tended to be at least 5ft 10in and weighed 185 pounds."

Fred Ropkey, a Marine Corps tanker, commanded Shermans during the Korean War. He talks about his impressions of driving a Sherman.

"We had pretty much of a non-standard way of driving the Shermans, particularly the ones we were using which had the dozer blades on them. We found it was much easier to drive standing up. You could clutch easier, get better leverage with the leg, and drive with your left arm in front of your face so you wouldn't knock your teeth out when you were bounding over things. The driver used the levers and normally steered with just one hand. Actually, in most cases you could steer a Sherman tank with one hand on one lever at a time. Of course on a hard pull, you might have to drop down the speed and make a hard turn with two hands. Most of the time when you weren't getting shot at, standing up seemed to be the preference for a lot of people, me included. I was taught this by some old guys, part of the old corps. When you've got a dozer blade on the front of your tank, you need all the visibility you can get."

Combat Driving

Driving any tank in combat requires many skills. Tank drivers must drive aggressively as well as defensively. They must constantly seek out hull-down positions to protect their vehicles from enemy fire, but at the same time allow their gun-

A close-up view of the Sherman tank steering levers. On the left of the floor is the clutch pedal. The accelerator pedal is on the right. Sherman tanks were very tiring vehicles to drive, especially when going cross-country. It helped to be young and strong.
Michael Green

ner to put maximum fire on the target. The working relationship between members of a tank crew must be as close as the working relationship between the old-time cavalry soldier and his horse. The relationship is not a matter of constant commands and countercommands but of reflexes. A good tank driver learns to anticipate the actions of his tank commander in a given situation so that the tank commander seldom has to issue detailed driving instructions during combat.

One of the basic combat lessons every tank driver learns is that you never cross over a hill or a ridge that outlines your vehicle against the sky. Instead, you find a saddle or draw that will get you to the same point over a slightly different route. When traveling cross-country where there is a wooded background, you must stay close to the edge of the woods. Overhanging branches offer concealment and the wooded background can help to break up the outline of your vehicle. When there is a choice between a trail and a cross-country route with about the same cover, the cross-country route is usually better. This is especially true during dry weather when dust clouds could give away the tank's position.

The shadows of buildings, trees, or other large objects were used as partial concealment. Tank commanders and tank drivers learned not to conceal their tanks behind a lone tree, a single clump of bushes, or any other easily identified point of concealment because the enemy's target identification would be much easier.

When fired upon, Sherman commanders and drivers were taught not to stop. If they were out in the open, they were told to speed up and take a course that would provide the greatest amount of cover. It was hoped that by using speed and taking advantage of any cover, a Sherman could present a more difficult target for the enemy gunners to spot and shoot at.

In all tanks, the driver's job is to constantly search for covered routes and positions to which he can move his vehicle if taken under enemy fire. During combat, tank drivers normally assist the vehicle's gunner and tank commander by observing targets and sensing fired rounds. Drivers also maintain the tank's position in formation and watch for visual signals, such as hand directions or signal flags. Drivers are responsible to the tank

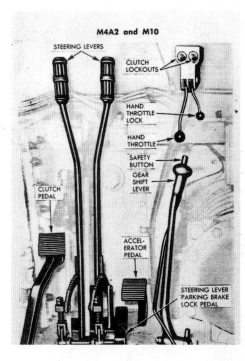

From a World War II tank manual comes this diagram of the driver's controls of an M4A2 Sherman with all its various components. Among the many things Sherman drivers were taught was to avoid obstacles if at all possible. If this couldn't be done, then an obstacle should be approached squarely. Tanks normally do not rush at an obstacle. A sufficiently low gear is used to insure continuous passage over the obstacle.

commander for the maintenance and refueling of the tank.

The assistant driver (or bow gunner) normally operated the bow .30cal machine gun mounted on the front hull of the vehicle. When not engaged in combat, the assistant driver helped the driver in the tank's maintenance and refueling. There were no dual controls for driving the tanks.

Tank Commander

The typical tank commander is responsible for the discipline and training of his crew. (In World War II, a US Army Sherman platoon had five vehicles). The tank commander is in charge of all assigned equipment, the reporting of logistical needs for his vehicle, and the tactical employment of his tank in combat. He also briefs his crew, directs the movement of the tank, submits all reports, and

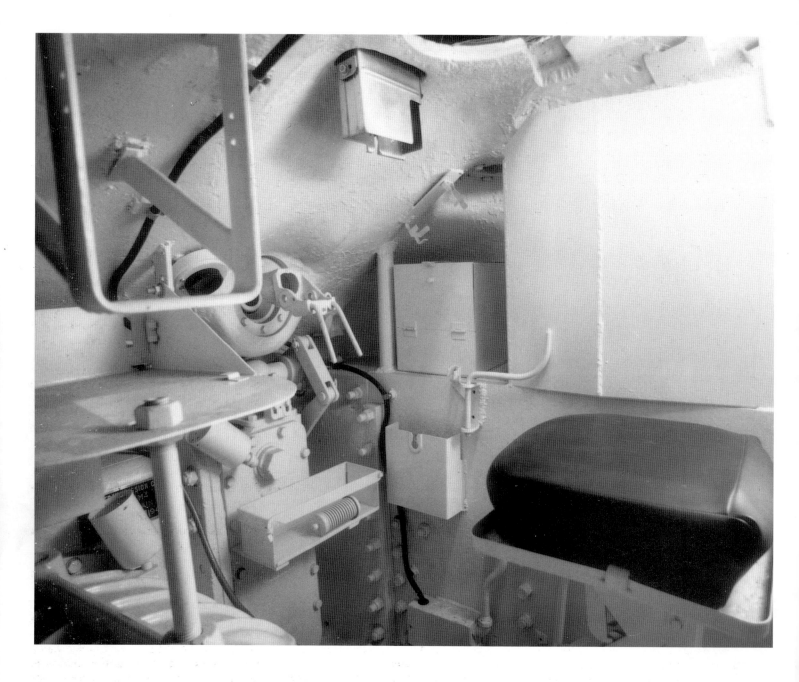

The Sherman tank's assistant-driver's position seen from the driver's position. Both the assistant driver's backrest and the .30cal machine gun are missing from this vehicle. Visible are the mounting brackets from the machine gun. *Michael Green*

supervises initial first-aid treatment and evacuation of wounded crew members. In combat, the tank commander is responsible for the aiming and firing of all weapons.

Gunner

The gunner's job on all tanks is to search for targets and aim and fire both the main gun and coaxial machine gun. He is responsible for the maintenance of the tank's armament and fire-control equipment and assists other crew members as needed. As the assistant tank commander, the gunner is responsible for the operation of the tank and performance of the crew in the absence of the tank commander.

Loader

The loader's job is to load the main gun and coaxial machine gun. He stows and cares for ammunition, maintains and operates the tank radio, and is trained as a replacement for the gunner. The loader assists other crew members as required and searches for targets until combat actually begins.

The loader's job is not an easy one. He works in a restricted space and normally cannot see the target after the engagement begins. The loader must remove a round from the rack, carefully guide the nose of the projectile into the breech, and shove it forward with sufficient force to trip the breechblock, seating the round in the chamber. All this has to be done quickly in the heat of battle.

Tank crews must be a tightly integrated team. Though all members have their primary duties, success depends on their

effectiveness as a crew. They must work together to maintain and service their tank and equipment, and they must function as one in combat. Crews in tanks normally cross-train so each member can function at any other position.

Communications

Sherman tank commanders and platoon leaders could choose from a number of different communications means including messenger, wire, visual, sound, or radio. An Army manual, dated January 12, 1942, listed the trumpet as an approved means of tank-to-tank communications. One might guess that the manual's authors spent many years in the cavalry. Trumpets were not normally part of the table of organization of any US Army tank unit.

The most secure means available for tank commanders and platoon leaders to transmit lengthy messages was to use a messenger. Commanders used messengers on foot, motorcycle, or jeep to deliver Sherman platoon fire plans and status reports to higher headquarters.

When companies set up tanks in initial defensive positions, assembly areas, or other static situations, crews could lay wire from one tank to another to communicate with the platoon leader's vehicle.

Crews could also connect field telephones to the wire allowing platoon leaders to communicate with observation posts or company command posts.

Visual signals consisted of either hand-and-arm or flag signals to control individual tank and platoon movements. Each tank was issued with a cased set of red, green, and yellow flags. Flags served as an extension of hand-and-arm signals when distance between vehicles became too great. Flashlights and other lights could also be used to transmit brief prearranged messages (for example, the identity of friendly units).

Lt. Col. Bill Hamberg, a World War II Sherman-battalion commander, remembers using nonverbal means to communicate.

"In early 1944, I was commanding a Tank Battalion in the 5th Armored Division located 'somewhere' in Southern England. We were a part of General Patton's 'phantom' Third Army and, consequently, were under strict radio silence. This meant that we had to train without radio communication. Instead, we used the 'two-letter code' hand or flag signals and we got good at it. So good, in fact, that later in combat we continued to use these same codes for most messages and orders. Of course now we were using

voice communications, but used the phonetic alphabet. I think we had codes for about 80 percent of the necessary messages. This was useful for security purposes, but more important to be sure that orders were not ambiguous or misunderstood. . .and to keep radio traffic to a minimum."

Crew members could also use pyrotechnic ammunition to illuminate an area at night or as a signal. The signals were generally used for friendly unit identification, maneuver element control, target marking, and location reports.

Whistles, horns, sirens, bells, voice amplifiers, and explosive devices could be used for audible communications. These means were mainly used to attract attention, transmit prearranged messages, and spread alarms.

The most flexible but least secure means of communication between tanks is the radio. The radio can quickly transmit information over long distances with great accuracy. However, radio signals are vulnerable to enemy interception or jamming. Tank platoons and individual tanks would normally use the radio when other means of communication couldn't be used.

In the rear of US Sherman turrets there was normally one of three different FM radio systems: the SCR508, the SCR528 or the SCR538. All of them had a top range of 10–20mi under favorable conditions; (line of sight). Under poor conditions, range could go down to under 5mi. Power for the radios came from the vehicle's batteries through a separate wiring system.

The SCR508 radio transmitter, which was combined with two radio receivers, was used in command tanks. With this setup, the company commander would have one receiver tuned to his company internal net and the other receiver tuned to the battalion net. The SCR528 radio, by contrast, had only one receiver and was found in platoon leaders' tanks where two-way communication was needed. The SCR538 radio had no transmitter at all, just a receiver. This type of

Knowing how to make good use of cover and concealment is important for any tank driver. It is impossible to put enough armor on a vehicle to stop penetration by all weapons. Pictured is an M4A3 Sherman tank at Fort Knox, Kentucky, demonstrating the correct way to use the cover of a tree and bushes. *US Army*

that could be many miles away. For those purposes, many commanders used the SCR245 or SCR506 AM radio sets. The SCR506 had a range of almost 50mi using voice communication and up to 100mi using a Morse key. In US tanks, the SCR245 and SCR506 were located in the hull.

For communication within tanks, each Sherman crew member had an intercom box (BC-606). Each crew member had a plug for a headphone set and a switch that allowed him to either broadcast on the tank's radio set or just on the intercom to the other crew members. For better vocal clarity, the commander was also provided with a small hand-held microphone or a throat microphone.

From the unpublished diary and letters of Lt. Col. Henry Gardiner comes this quote.

"For some time ours was the only medium tank outfit in this operation but there are now several, although I don't believe any of them have been committed as yet. During this past battle, I was in or on my tank most of the time. You use a throat microphone on the interphone and radio. In the excitement at one point I forgot to switch from interphone to radio and learned later that all of my fire directions to the 75mm gunner to fire on some tanks were going out over the air. My radio is tied into units back of the lines so they were getting a play-by-play description of what was going on."

For two-way communication between tank crews and infantry on foot following or directing tanks in combat, there was also the AN/VRC-3, a take-off on the well-known SCR300 Walkie Talkie. It was mounted inside the Sherman turret, something like a modern cordless phone system. Another method of tank-to-ground communication featured an RC-298 intercom extension kit fitted in a small box welded to the right rear of the Sherman hull. If an infantryman wanted to talk to the Sherman crew, he would walk to the rear of the tank, open the lid on the small intercom box, take out the phone, and make his request known.

Normally, US tankers wore a padded composite-fiber crash helmet (copied from pre-war football helmets) fastened together with narrow straps of leather or elastic webbing material. Inserted within this crash helmet were earplugs or small round earphones for the crew member to listen to either the vehicle's intercom sys-

setup was for tanks that did not have a need to send messages to anybody. This was later changed to a normal setup with a transmitter when it was quickly realized that it could be the tank without the transmitter that would first spot the enemy.

Some tank-battalion commanders not only had to communicate with their lower level subordinates in the field but also deal with division-level command posts

Normally located in the rear turret bulge of all Sherman tanks was a push-button high frequency (FM), voice-operated radio. Unlike the solid-state transistors everybody uses today, these radios were filled with fragile vacuum tubes. The radio set pictured in this M4A1 tank is an SCR528 normally found in platoon leader's tanks.
Michael O'Brien

tem or the radio. To transmit, the Sherman crew member wore a throat mic which consisted of two small button shaped devices held against the larynx by means of a combination elastic band and metal clip fastened around the throat. When the operator spoke, the vocal chords set up a vibration in the transmitter directly instead of through the air, as with an ordinary mic. Neither the earplugs or earphones for the tanker's helmets or the throat mic were popular among Sherman tankers as they became

very uncomfortable very fast. There was also a lip microphone available for use by tankers, which was unpopular and seldom seen in the field.

Because the crash helmet offered no protection from bullets or shell fragments, some Sherman crew members also wore a foam-padded set of earphones (first available in 1944) that could be fitted under the standard steel helmet. Most tankers who didn't have access to the foam-padded earphone sets would merely take the liner out of their steel helmet and jam the outer steel pot over the leather crash helmet.

Reprinted with permission from the *Marine Corps Gazette* Magazine is an example of what you might hear between Shermans during combat. It was recorded by a US Navy destroyer lying offshore during the battle for Guam in 1944. The destroyer made a recording of the radio communication between Marine tanks

engaged in a fight against a background of machine gun fire, mortar explosions, and engine noise. An expurgated version of their words is repeated here. The men's voices can be imagined ranging from flat and authoritative during moments of sulfurous stress to almost unintelligible male soprano during great excitement.

"'This is Red Two, Red One. Heartburn says that he is ready to start shooting at those pillboxes.'

"'Tell Heartburn I can't receive him. You will have to relay. Tell him to give us a signal and we'll spot for him.'

"'Red Two, wilco.'
* * *
"'Heartburn, raise your fire. You're right into us.'

"'That's not Heartburn, Red Two. That's a high-velocity gun from our left rear. I heard it whistle. Red One, out.'

"'Red Three, this is Red One. Can

This photo, taken inside a World War II
Sherman tank, shows the tank commander's
position, with his overhead hatch, and the
gunner, who sits right below and in front of
the commander. The gunner is looking
through his periscope, which includes a
telescopic sight within it. *US Army*

you see that gun that's shooting at us?'

"'Red One, I think that's our own gunfire.'

"'Goddammit, it's not, I tell you. It's a high-velocity gun and not a howitzer. Investigate over there on your left. But watch out for the infantry; they're right in there somewhere. Red Two, tell Heartburn "Down Fifty, Left Fifty"'

"'Red Two, wilco.'

"'Red Three, what are you doing? Go southwest.'

"'I am heading southwest, Red One.'

"'For Christ's sake, get oriented. I can see you, Red Three. You are heading northwest. Fox Love with hard left brake. Cross the road and go back up behind that house.'

"'But—'

"'I don't know why I bother with you, Red Three. Yellow One, take charge of Red Three and get him squared away. And get that gun; it's too close.'

"'Red One from Red Two, Heartburn wants to know if we are the front lines.'

"'Tell him, "Christ, yes." We're plenty front right now.'

"'This is Red Two. Artillery on the way.'

"'Red One, wilco.'
* * *

"'Red One from Yellow One. I can see some Japs setting up a machine gun about 100 yards to my right.'

"'Those are our troops, Yellow One. Don't shoot in there.'

"'The man at my telephone—I think he's an officer—says we have no troops in there.'

"'Yellow Two, go over there and investigate. Don't shoot at them; that man at your telephone probably doesn't know where the troops are. If they're Japs, run over them.'

"'Yellow One, wilco.'
* * *

"'Go ahead, Yellow Two. What in God's name are you waiting for?'

"'I'm up as far as I can go and still depress my machine guns.'

"'The hell with the machine guns. I told you to run over them. Run over them, goddammit; obey your orders.'

"'Yellow Two, wilco.'
* * *

"'Yellow One, what have you to report on that machine gun?"

"'Red One, a Jap stood up and threw a hand grenade at us so I gave him a squirt.'

"'Did you run over that gun like I told you?'

"'No. Red One, we put an HE in it and wrecked it.'

"'Cheerist, won't you people ever learn to conserve your ammunition?'
* * *

"'Red One from Green Two. I'm stuck between two trees.'

"'Green Three stand by him. After the infantry has cleared up around there, get your assistant driver out and tow him clear.'

"'Green Three, wilco.'

"'While you're waiting, Green Three, keep an eye on that house on your right. I see troops coming out of there stuffing bottles in their shirts.'

"'Can I send my assistant driver over to investigate?'

"'Stay in your tank. That's only Saki.'

"'Yellow One from Red Three, where are you going?'
* * *

"'Red One from Green Four. I am moving out to take a pillbox the infantry pointed out. I will take care of it and let them catch up.'

"'Where is it, Green Four?'

"'In that clump of bushes to my right. Can you see it? It is all right to fire?'

"'Wait, Green Four.'

"'Green Four, wilco.'

"'Green Four, you'd better not fire. The 4th Marines are over there somewhere. Run up on the box and turn around on it.'

"'It's one of those coconut log things. It looks like it might be too strong to squash. Is it all right if I fire in the slit?'

"'Affirmative, but be careful.'

"'Wilco.'
* * *

"'Red One, this is Hairless. We've got some Japs bottled up in two caves in Target Area Four Baker. We'd like you to leave two tanks to watch them.'

"'You know damn well that's the infantry's work. We're a mobile outfit, not watchdogs. Put your saki drinkers in there.'

"'OK, Harry.'

"'Red One, out.'
* * *

"'All tanks, start 'em up. Move out now. Guide right and form a shallow right echelon. As soon as we hit the flat ground around the airfield, spread out to one hundred fifty yard interval. All right, move out, move out.'"

Chapter 5

Firepower

Prior to the war, tanks were seen mostly as an infantry support weapon and machine guns were the primary tank weapon. After the German invasion of Poland in 1939 and France in 1940, the US Army realized the Germans were using tanks with cannons as large as 75mm. This forced the US Army to field tanks with comparable firepower. The end result was the development of the Sherman mounting a 75mm cannon in a rotating turret.

It is important to understand at this point that not all tank guns are created equal. Merely because a tank cannon has a bore diameter of 75mm (2.92in) doesn't mean it will have the same performance characteristics as a 75mm gun found on another country's tank. More important in determining the effectiveness of a tank

The crew of this Sherman tank load a variety of equipment onboard their vehicle. Besides the 75mm main gun round being handed to the tanker on the left, the tanker on the right holds both smoke and antipersonnel grenades. The masking tape strips on top of the tankers' crash helmets are used to hold the intercom cords seen hanging from their helmets. *US Army*

gun in combat are its design, the materials used in building it, how it was built, the type of ammunition used, how long the barrel is, and what type of fire control system is used to fire it.

German industry before and during the war had the best machine tools in the world. Its gauges and precision measuring devices were far better than anything American manufacturers had. At the time, German mechanics were also the world's best trained. The combination of these elements allowed German manufacturers to build more powerful and longer ranged tank guns, more effective ammunition, and more accurate optical sighting systems.

The Soviet tank designers, well aware of their disadvantages in the designing and building of tank guns, decided early in the war to build and mount the biggest guns they could fit in their armored vehicles. They thought the larger guns would make up for the guns' shortcomings. As an example the T34, the classic Soviet tank of the war, went from mounting a 76.2mm gun to an 85mm gun. Yet, while their tank guns were bigger and fired a larger shell than the 75mm gun of the German Panther tank, they still could not meet the same performance standards of

the Panther's gun because of poorer gun construction and substandard ammunition.

In contrast, the American and British military leaders continuously underestimated what they needed to defeat German armor. Even near the end of the war when both American and British military leaders had realized their earlier mistakes and rushed new heavy tanks with bigger guns into production, they still lagged at least two years behind the leading edge of German tank gun design.

The primary effectiveness of tank cannons on modern armored vehicles like the American M1 Abrams is gauged by its ability to defeat the armor protection of other tanks. When the Sherman was designed in 1941, the main purpose of the vehicle as envisioned by American military leaders was as a deep attack (exploitation) weapon. An example of this train of thought can be found in a US Army field manual of April 1943.

"The ultimate objective of the armored division is vital rear installations. These are attacked less with cannon than with the crushing power of the tank and with its machine guns. The main purpose of the tank cannon is to permit the tank to overcome enemy resistance and reach the vital rear areas."

To allow the Shermans to fulfill their primary mission as weapons of exploitation, the US Army fielded highly specialized vehicles known as tank destroyers. Their job was to destroy enemy tanks that would try to stop the Shermans from plunging deep behind enemy lines.

This concept had evolved from pre-war American military thinking about anti-tank warfare. While the doctrine was a matter of dispute both before and during the war, the eventual result was the production of fully tracked, lightly armored, high-speed vehicles mounting the largest antitank weapons then in service. At least two models of these tank destroyers wound up being built on the Sherman chassis. (See Chapter 9.)

75mm Cannon

The 75mm gun mounted in the Sherman was considered by soldiers of many armies to be a first-class weapon for the roles for which it was intended. Even as an antitank weapon, the Sherman's 75mm gun proved to be more than a match for the Mark III and Mark IV tanks it was designed to counter. The American military's failure to plan for improved German tanks was not the failure of the Sherman's designers.

The 75mm gun in the Sherman was technically known as the M3. It was broadly based on a 75mm field gun that was introduced into French military service in the early 1900s. At the time the French 75, as it was known, was the first gun to feature a recoil system. It had a long barrel and high muzzle velocity (for its day), and saw heavy action during World War I. After that war, the French 75 was built under license for the US Army.

When the call went out for mounting a 75mm gun in the M3 medium tank and later the Sherman, Watervliet Arsenal (a government owned plant) quickly redesigned the American version of the French 75 to fit the gun mounts on the American tanks.

Much like a large rifle barrel, the Sherman's 75mm gun tube was formed out of one large piece of alloy steel. From the firing chamber forward, the gun tube was rifled with grooves having a uniform right-hand twist.

The breech mechanism of the 75mm gun consisted of the breech ring, breechblock, and the breech operating mecha-

nism. The Sherman's breechblock was of the horizontal sliding type. The upper front edge of the breechblock was beveled to force a 75mm round into the firing chamber as the breech closed. A hole in the center of the breechblock housed the percussion mechanism, firing spring, and firing spring retainer. On the left side of the breechblock were the trigger, sear, and sear spring. On the right side were the cocking lever, cocking lever shaft, and cocking lever spring.

The breech face was recessed on each side to receive the lips of the cartridge-case extractors when the breech was closed. The extractors were short heavy levers supported vertically in the breech ring. The side of each extractor had an inner projecting lip that fitted between the rim of the cartridge case and the rear face of the gun tube when the breech was closed.

The 75mm gun tube and components were supported and aligned in their mount by means of a machined surface on the rear of the gun tube. Lugs were provided on the bottom of the breech ring to support the operating shaft and cranks which operated the 75mm gun breech mechanism. A horizontal hole in the lower part of the breech ring housed the closing spring mechanism.

Firing the Cannon

To open the breech of the Sherman's 75mm gun tube you had to grasp and pull to the rear and then push on the operating handle. As the breechblock opened, the trunnions of the extractors were forced forward into the trunnion seats. This would lock the breechblock in the open position. When a round of ammunition was loaded into the firing chamber, the rear rim of the loaded round would contact with the lip of the extractors and push them forward, the breech would then automatically close. At the same time, the breechblock moved sideward into the closed position driven

Pictured inside an M4A1 Sherman tank is the breech end of a 75mm gun with a dummy 75mm round inserted halfway into the firing chamber. At this point in an operational Sherman tank, the loader pushes the round completely into the firing chamber. The breechblock (missing in this vehicle) automatically closes behind the main gun round. *Michael Green*

Removed from the turret of an M4A1 Sherman tank is the 75mm gun, technically known as the M3. Visible is the gun's breech end. Surrounding the gun breech is the body guard or recoil guard. To the left of the gun is the mount for the coaxial .30cal machine gun. *Michael Green*

by the force of the expanding closing springs.

When the firing pin struck the primer of the loaded 75mm round in the firing chamber, the gun would go off. Recoil moved the 75mm gun tube to the rear. The recoil motion operated a cam that opened the breech. As the breechblock became fully opened and cleared the rear of the 75mm cartridge case, the extractor lips rotated to the rear as the extractor trunnions moved forward in curved extractor grooves. The lips of the extractors pulled the case from the firing chamber and then ejected it from the gun's breech ring.

Recoil Mechanism

The Sherman gun mount was fitted with a hydraulic mechanism to absorb the recoil from firing the cannon. The recoil mechanism consisted of a cradle, the 75mm gun tube, recoil cylinder, and counter-recoil spring. The recoil cylinder is keyed to the 75mm gun tube near the front of the cradle. The counter-recoil spring is coiled around the gun tube be-

tween the recoil piston and the rear of the cradle. When ready for operation, the recoil cylinder was completely full of hydraulic fluid.

As the 75mm gun moved to the rear in recoil, the hydraulic fluid was forced from the rear of the recoil piston to the front of the recoil piston. At the same time, the counter-recoil spring compressed. The inside of the cradle was tapered inward from front to rear so the clearance between the piston and cradle was greatest at the beginning of the recoil. As the 75mm gun neared the end of its recoil, the throttling of the hydraulic fluid's flow by the taper caused it to damp the gun's rearward movement.

When the recoil was absorbed, the compressed counter-recoil spring expanded, moving the 75mm gun forward. This movement forced the fluid from the front of the recoil piston to the rear of the piston. Near the end of this counter recoil movement, an enlarged portion of the gun tube entered the buffer chamber in the front of the recoil cylinder. The movement of fluid out of the buffer chamber was thereby restricted and provided in turn a cushioning effect as the restricted flow eased the 75mm gun back into its mount without undue shock to the turret.

Armor Penetration

All tanks fired AP rounds that depended on kinetic energy to destroy ene-

my tanks. Kinetic energy penetration is produced by propelling a round of great mass and strength at very high velocities. Upon impact, the slug or penetrator is supposed to puncture the armor plate and ricochet within the enemy tank.

The best way to increase the kinetic energy of a projectile is to increase its velocity. The Sherman's M3 75mm cannon had a relatively poor muzzle velocity and armor-piercing performance. The muzzle velocity of an M61 round being fired out of the M3 cannon was only 2030fps. By contrast, the armor-piercing round fired by the Panther's 75mm gun achieved 3,675fps. The Germans also had superior ammunition and sighting telescopes, so it was a very one-sided match between Shermans and the Panther and Tiger tanks.

Cpl. James A. Miller, a Sherman gunner, was frustrated by the lack of muzzle velocity in his wartime report.

"I have been in combat several times in a tank and I have found out it is silly to try to fight the German tank. One morning in Puffendorf, Germany, about daylight I saw German tanks coming across the field toward us; we all opened fire on them, but we had just about as well have fired our shots straight up in the air for all the good we could do. Every round would bounce off and wouldn't do a bit of damage. I fired at one 800yd away, he had his side toward me. I hit him from the lap of the turret to the bottom and from the front of the tank to the back directly in the side but he never halted. I fired one hundred and eighty four rounds at them and I hit at least five of them several times. In my opinion if we had a gun with plenty of muzzle velocity we would have wiped them out. We out-gunned them but our guns were worthless."

Pfc. Raymond E. Fleming, Sherman driver, and T/Sgt. George C. Maurer, gunner, related this story in a field report.

"It happened just north of Krefeld, Germany. We were advancing at a good rate of speed when the platoon leader, whose gunner I happened to be, spotted

A tank crew from the 5th AD, training in the United States, loads their M4A3 Sherman tank with ammunition. The blue-tipped rounds are HE shells; the black-tipped rounds are AP shells. The photo also shows a long belt of .30cal machine gun ammunition being loaded into the vehicle's turret. *US Army*

STOWAGE FOR MEDIUM TANK M4 SERIES

A display of the typical stowage for the Sherman medium tank M4 series was constructed at Aberdeen Proving Ground, Maryland, as a training aid. In this picture you can see the wide variety of items that have to be cramped into a typical tank. Not shown are the dozens of other items that Sherman tankers normally added to their vehicles to make their lives a little more comfortable. These extra items were usually hung from the turret or stowed on the rear hull engine deck of the vehicle. *Patton Museum*

a Jerry tank. [*Jerry* was slang for German.]

"From the distance he said it was a Mark V. I bounced two off it at 750yd, and he put two right through the front of ours. I should think that would be enough proof, that they have a better tank and also a better gun."

Ammunition

The M3 cannon mounted in the Sherman could fire three different types of rounds: high-explosive (HE), white-phosphorous (WP), and armor-piercing (AP).

The most important and most often used by Shermans during the war was the M48 HE shell. The typical target for a Sherman tended to be an antitank gun or infantry. Against enemy personnel and material targets which were vulnerable to blast effect and fragmentation, the Sherman's M48 HE shell was very effective. The projectile itself was made out of

forged steel with comparatively thin walls and contained 1.5lb of TNT.

The M48 HE shell could be fitted with a super-quick or a delayed, point-detonating fuse. The super-quick fuse is so sensitive that the shell detonates immediately on impact. Therefore, when striking armor plate, a gun shield or a building, the shell will burst before it can penetrate. The super-quick burst was effective against enemy personnel in the open, however.

Using the 0.05sec delay action on the M48 HE shell results in the shell penetrating before bursting when it strikes light armor, gun shields, or buildings. If the shell strikes the ground, it ricochets, travels 20–25yd beyond the point of impact and then bursts about 10ft in the air. Because of the downspray from the burst in the air, a ricochet burst has a devastating effect on enemy personnel who do

Often confused by American soldiers with the Tiger I heavy tank, this destroyed German Mark IV medium tank lies abandoned in a farmer's field on February 11, 1945. Armed with a long-barrel 75mm gun in this version, the Mark IV was comparable to the Sherman tank in most of its operational characteristics. Almost 9,000 various types of Mark IV tanks came off German production lines before the end of World War II. *US Army*

not have overhead cover. Even though the AP round was more effective against other tanks, the M48 HE round was often effective against German tanks. The following quote is from a book published shortly after the war by the 3rd AD entitled *Spearhead in the West*.

"At Pont Hebert, the fighting was intense. The 3rd Battalion of the 33rd AR lost all of its command tanks, including the tank of Lt. Col. Sam Hogan. But there were victories too: during their first 15min of combat, a tank crew commanded by Sgt. Dean Balderson knocked out three German Mark IVs. Balderson pulled out of a small orchard at dawn, and his gunner, Cpl. 'Swede' Anderson, immediately spotted the enemy. Four Kraut tanks were in position on the road ahead, their guns pointed in the opposite direction and evidently waiting for another company of the 33rd to advance.

"Anderson's first round, an HE, caught the nearest Mark IV flush on the turret, and things began to happen. The enemy tank blew up in a sudden gust of flame and black smoke! Immediately afterward the remaining Jerry vehicles were alert and moving. Excited, Anderson called for an AP shell, but his loader, Pfc. Bill Wilson, threw in a second HE. This shell duplicated the first and a second Mark IV blew up. Wilson found an AP round for the third shot and his gunner sent this projectile crashing through for number three. Three enemy battlewagons in less than fifteen minutes of combat! Sgt. Balderson and his crew decided that was a soft snap. Another week of fighting convinced them that it was just the opposite."

The Sherman's WP round was the M89. Nicknamed the Willy Peter, the M89 WP round was used to either screen the tank or to mark enemy targets for other vehicles. In the 4th AD many tankers kept a WP round in the breech ready for action. Since it could be used to mark a target, screen a vehicle with smoke, or even kill.

WP is nasty stuff. Phosphorous will burn through the skin and flesh and cannot be put out by water. Its burns are slow to heal. WP rounds could be fired into wooded areas to produce both casualty and incendiary effect. The trick for the Sherman gunner was to fire at the treetops so that phosphorous particles would scatter and fall. WP rounds could be used to burn thickets and brush.

WP rounds could also be effective against tanks and other materials that are likely to be oily. The burning phosphorous ignited oil and grease, creating a surface fire. It may burn the target or the fumes and smoke may enter an enemy tank through seams and joints forcing the crew to abandon their vehicle and thus neutralizing it.

In urban combat (city fighting), WP rounds could be fired into the ground floor of buildings. As the smoke and fumes lifted to the upper stories, the occupants would be driven out. The smoke and burning particles of WP were also effective against caves or fortifications which couldn't be attacked in any other way.

The Sherman's AP round was the M61. This round had been designed to have an HE element within it, but production problems caused it to be issued without this HE element until the very end of the war.

AP projectiles having no HE filler are called shot. The shot may be solid or it may have a small hollow cavity in its body. Those AP projectiles filled with an HE element were fitted with a base-detonating fuse having a delay action that would burst after penetration of enemy armor plate. With the HE element, the M61 AP round became the M61 AP-HE round. The M61 AP was designed primarily for the destruction of armored vehicles.

While in combat, Shermans normally carried more rounds than they were designed for, but the original complement of ammunition was supposed to be 97 rounds of various types for the M4 tanks with a welded hull and 90 rounds for the M4s with the cast hull. These rounds were divided between the vehicle's turret and hull. The turret of the welded-hull Sherman had carrying spaces for 20 rounds. Twelve of these were stored around the lower turret basket wall, with eight more in a ready-rack under the 75mm gun. There were stowage racks on either side of the Sherman hull. Fifteen rounds were stored in a rack next to the loader's position. On the commander's side of the hull, there was stowage rack space for 32 rounds. Located behind the bow gunners was a storage compartment for 30 rounds.

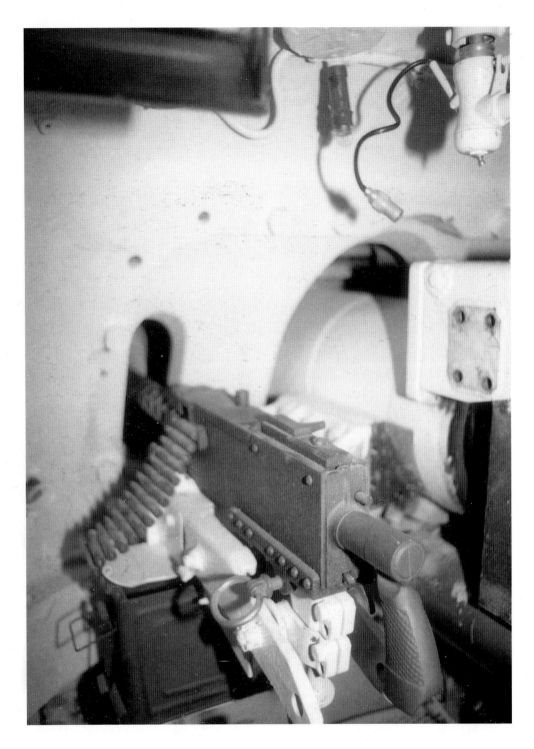

Located alongside the main gun in all Sherman tanks was a coaxial .30cal machine gun. It was used on any and all targets that didn't require the firing of the main gun. Of the three machine guns normally found on Shermans, the coaxial was used the most often. *Michael Green*

the day. This was a big job and had to be done when you were tired out—GI's are clever at getting out of BIG JOBS. This was corrected by requiring every weapon to be fired (toward the enemy) at the start of the day. The command was 'Dirty All Bores' (DOG BAKER in our code). Now there was no gain in not firing your weapons the rest of the day. Consequently, we used a lot of ammunition, but we never ran out and we didn't bring any home!"

Machine Guns

Besides the 75mm main gun, the typical Sherman was fitted with at least three machine guns. There was a coaxial .30cal machine gun mounted to fire alongside the main gun. It was used on unarmored vehicles or infantry. It was fired by a foot switch operated by the Sherman gunner. Another .30cal machine gun was mounted in the right front hull in a ball mount operated by the assistant driver. Some tankers considered the bow .30cal a waste of time as it was so hard to sight. The only way it could be aimed was by the use of tracer ammunition. Other tankers saw the Sherman's bow .30cal as a useful means of at least keeping the enemy's head down in combat.

Early prototype Sherman tanks had been armed with twin fixed .30cal machine guns in the front hull. Surprisingly, these machine guns could be fired accurately as long as the tank had room to move. But, due to an early-war machinegun shortage, these weapons were deleted from production Shermans.

Located on the turret near the commander's cupola of the Sherman was mounted a .50cal machine gun. The basic model used on the Sherman was the air-cooled M2 HB (Heavy Barrel). The M2 HB .50cal machine gun has a barrel length of 45in and weighs in at about 84lb without tripod. It can fire at selectable rates of 450 to 550 rounds per minute. Its maximum effective range is a little over 1200yd.

Muzzle velocity of the several types of ammunition fired by the M2 HB .50cal machine gun is about 2900fps, enough to destroy lightly armored enemy vehicles.

Mounted on the Sherman, the .50cal machine gun tended to be used on almost anything that didn't require the firing of the 75mm main gun. Lt. Col. William Hamberg remembers:

"The .50cal machine gun was con-

Lt. Col. William Hamberg remembers:

"Firing of weapons in combat is difficult to control. Men are reluctant to fire at anything that they can't see, consequently, 'reconnaissance-by-fire,' an essential technique of tank attacks, was not a voluntary action. Why?...We soon found out the reason: If you fired your weapon, it must be cleaned at the end of

stantly fired at anything that could hide a German antitank weapon of any sort. In farm country the machine gun was always fired at large and small haystacks. If the .50cal ammo hit something hard inside the haystack and bounced off, it would be immediately fired upon with the 75mm main gun. We also liked the fact that the .50cal machine gun could fire an incendiary round, which was excellent for setting wooden barns on fire."

When ambushed by dug-in German infantry armed with portable antitank weapons, the .50cal machine gun dislodged the enemies from their hiding places. From the book *Paths of Armor*, a history of the 5th AD, the following excerpt describes a combat action in Germany in 1945:

"Every gun of the assaulting tanks shot at once. In Molnar's tank, Pvt. Richard Vicknair loaded the 76, then jumped to the .50cal machine gun in his turret to spray the Germans. Molnar's gunner, Cpl. Elmer E. Huffstetter, purposely shot short of the foxholes, which sent projectiles flying into the dirt in front of the holes and down inside them, killing the occupants. T/4 Charles Stoeckeln, Molnar's driver, was doing the work of three men in the front of the tank. He drove, leaned over to fire the assistant driver's machine gun (.30cal), and handed up ammunition out of the spare racks to the men in the turret behind him."

The machine guns on Shermans could be used for ricochet fire. Although this type of fire is not accurate, the psychological effect on enemy troops is considerable. Ricochet fire in street fighting keeps down enemy sniper fire. Machine gun fire can be delivered around corners by ricocheting it from buildings, walls, or fences.

Both .30 and .50cal machine fire from a Sherman could be used to remove hasty mines (especially wooden ones) from hard surfaced areas such as roads. The fire either exploded the mine or physically swept it from the road.

When not in use, the .50cal machine gun was stowed on the rear of some Sherman turrets with the barrel removed.

British and Canadian tank units did not favor the mounting of the .50cal machine gun on the Sherman turret. More often, British Shermans tended to use the .30cal machine gun on a turret mount. Some American Shermans also had .30cal machine guns fitted.

Shermans normally carried about 500 rounds of .50cal ammunition, 5,000 rounds of .30cal ammunition and a number of 30-round clips of .45cal ammunition for on-board sub-machine guns.

Sighting Systems

The first model M4 and M4A1 Shermans were fitted only with an M4 periscope incorporating the M38A1 telescope sight mounted on the front of the

From behind the assistant driver's seat of an Israeli Army Sherman tank is the receiver and trigger grip of a .30cal machine gun that was mounted in the front hull of most Shermans. Having no sighting device, the only way the gun could be aimed was by watching where the tracer-ammo went. Although inaccurate, the gun was used most often to keep the enemy's heads down.
Michael Green

The early model Sherman tanks like this M4A1 kept most of their 75mm main gun ammunition in the hull-mounted stowage boxes. Unfortunately, this type of stowage arrangement meant that an enemy antitank round entering the hull would probably set off the onboard ammo supply.
Michael Green

turret. This periscope sight proved to be unreliable for aiming the cannon because the linkage arm connecting the sight to the gun's elevating mechanism would work itself out of adjustment after hard use.

In 1943 Shermans were fitted with a direct three-power telescope sight known as the M55. (The M55 was later superseded by the M70F.) The original Sherman periscope incorporating the telescope M38A1 was kept as a backup sight on all Sherman models.

1st Lt. David O. Craycraft, 3rd TB, 66th AR, compares the sights on the Sherman to those of a German Panther tank.

"The sights on the Mark V tank are better than sights used on the American M4 because they seem to be clearer, are adjustable, and are more powerful. Also, range estimation can be obtained with the German sight. However, when the Mark V is buttoned up, the limited view is a decided disadvantage over the American sight."

To protect the new M55 direct-sight telescope mounted on the Sherman, the front gun shield was redesigned and extended to cover not only the telescope on the right of the main gun but the .30cal coaxial machine gun mounted on the left of the front gun shield.

Traversing Controls

Based on a number of US Army manuals. Some of the following text describes fire-control components of the Sherman tank armed with either the 75mm or 76mm gun.

How fast a tank can shoot depends on the machinery for traversing and elevating the vehicle's main gun and on its loader and gunner.

In the Sherman, and most other American tanks, the tank gun and coaxial machine gun were mounted in the turret and were traversed by rotating the turret. For slow, small movements the gunner had a hand-operated control or manual traverse; for fast, large movements he had a power-operated traversing mechanism.

The power traverse was hydraulically operated. A variable displacement electric pump furnished the pressure. A motor geared to the turret ring applied the energy necessary to rotate the turret in a clockwise or counterclockwise direction at variable speeds dependent on pump pressure.

The amount and direction of this

pressure was controlled by the setting of the power traverse control handle. The control handle was held in the neutral position by a spring. When it was released, it returned to the vertical position and stopped the rotation of the turret. The tank commander could traverse the turret independently from the gunner by a dual or remote control. The tank commander's control would override the gunner's control.

The gunner could also turn the turret manually, through a complete circle, with a manual traversing control handle. The gunner rotated the manual control in the direction the turret was to be traversed. The brake on the manual traversing control handle prevented accidental rotation of the turret. The gunner had to release the brake by squeezing the release lever before he could traverse the turret manually.

The power- and manual-traverse mechanisms both worked on the same pinion gear, but only one could be engaged at a time. The shift lever engages either the power-traverse motor or the manual-traverse system. Moving the shift lever down engaged the manual mechanism. Moving the shift lever up engaged the power-traverse motor. The power traverse had to be fully engaged before attempting power operation or the mechanism would be damaged.

The turret had a lock that prevented any turret rotation by locking the turret to the turret ring gear. The lock's primary purpose was to reduce the strain and wear on the traversing mechanism by preventing unnecessary turret movement when the tank was in motion. To lock the turret, a crew member turned the turret lock handle to the vertical position and let it slip into the IN position. The lock handle automatically returned to the horizontal position. On occasion it was necessary to slightly rotate the manual traverse control handle to allow the turret lock to engage. To disengage the turret lock a crew member turned the lock handle one quarter to the right (to a vertical position), pulled it out as far as possible, and returned it to the horizontal position.

In combat, the very fast turret traverse system on the Sherman sometimes allowed it to get in a shot or two at enemy tanks before they could turn their own turrets around to fire. But generally, while German tanks had a much slower traverse, they were normally fast enough to track any Sherman except those operating at very high speed or very close in.

Elevation Controls

The Sherman had two means of changing the elevation of the cannon. One was a manual elevating handwheel geared directly to the gun mount. The other means was the gyrostabilizer control, an electric-hydraulic mechanism that maintained the gun at a preset elevation, within the limits, independent of the tank's motion. The gunner disengaged the manual elevating gears before attempting to use the gyrostabilizer; this was done by means of the elevating shift lever.

The gunner elevated or depressed the gun tube manually by turning the elevating handwheel; this turned an elevating pinion gear in mesh with the elevating rack on the gun mount. When the gunner rotated the elevating handwheel, the elevating rack moved up or down elevating or depressing the gun tube and gun trunnion. The gun muzzle was elevated by turning the handwheel to the rear (toward the gunner); it was depressed by rotating the handwheel forward (away from the gunner).

When both the manual and gyrostabilizer elevation controls were out of action on the Sherman, there was still at least one other backup system demonstrated by Sgt. William Bolich of the 751st TB, during the fighting in Italy in 1943. His story is described in the files of the US Army Center for Military History.

"Sgt. William Bolich had concealed his tank in a house where he could cover the road into Carano. While he was observing from the turret, an enemy shell struck the house bringing down part of the stone and masonry wall. Sergeant Bolich was struck in the back by a piece of concrete and a second block damaged the elevating mechanism of the 75mm gun so that the muzzle could not be raised. In spite of his injured back, Sergeant Bolich crawled out of the turret and propped up the barrel of the gun sufficiently to allow the gunner to fire. In the course of the day, the damaged M4 knocked out three Mark IV tanks and effectively stopped the armored attack."

Gyrostabilizer

Ahead of its time, the Sherman crew had the ability to aim and fire their 75mm main guns somewhat accurately (in ele-

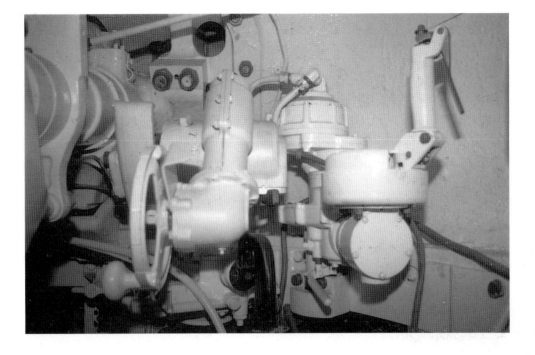

vation only) while on the move. This feature, which tanks built by other countries didn't have, was provided by a device known as a gyrostabilizer. Consisting of a very small gyro attached to the 75mm gun mount, every time the tank went up or down when moving, the gyro sensed any deviation from where the gun was being aimed at. Corrections were fed to a small elevation sensor which formed part of the gyrostabilizer system. The sensor returned the gun via a hydraulic cylinder approximately where it had been originally laid by the Sherman gunner. It tended to eliminate extremely jerky movements caused by the movement of the tank when viewed through the gunner optics. However, even with the gyrostabilizer, the 75mm gun would not hold constantly on a target. The Sherman gunner tended to use his manually-operated handwheel to re-aim the gun if the target moved or his tank changed direction. Many 76mm Shermans were not equipped with a gyrostabilizer.

Firing the gun while moving required close teamwork between the driver and gunner. The driver had to move the vehicle at a constant speed; acceleration and deceleration upset the action of the stabilizer. The driver had to move in a straight line, otherwise the gun moved as the tank turned. The driver had to warn the gunner when rough terrain was to be crossed so the gunner would not fight the gun before firing (attempt to keep it on target by

A close-up photo of the Sherman tank gunner's controls. The horizontal wheel on the left is the elevating handwheel for the tank's main gun. The black hand grip in the bottom center is the hydraulic turret traverse control handle. The hand grip on the upper right is the manual traverse drive handle. By turning the hand grip on the manual traverse drive handle in a circular motion, the Sherman turret could be slowly turned. *Michael Green*

spinning the elevating handwheel), but wait until a constant speed could be regained and the action of the stabilizer had smoothed out.

Because gyrostabilizers were such delicate mechanisms, they often did not work in the field. Sometimes they needed so much adjustment to function properly that crews tended not to use them unless ordered to.

Lt. Col. William A. Hamberg remembers:

"We had a stabilizer on the Sherman tank, but the tankers thought it was useless. When training for combat, we always insisted that the lead tank would be one whose stabilizer was working. This was our standard operating procedure [SOP]. After a few days of combat, I suddenly realized that all of the stabilizers were down. Nobody wanted to be the lead tank! When we changed the SOP to remove this requirement, stabilizers began to work again!"

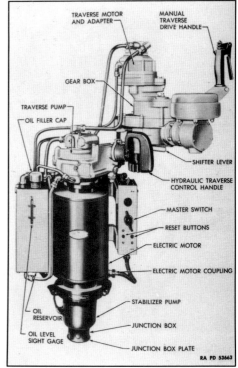

This close-up photo of an Israeli-modified Sherman tank, belonging to a private collector, shows a number of interesting upper turret details common to most Sherman tanks. Fitted with the US-designed late-war improved vision cupola on the left of the photo, it replaced the older split circular hatch found on early Shermans. In front of the cupola (on the far left) is a travel lock for the .50cal machine gun barrel. Next to the travel lock is the gunner's periscope. Next to the gunner's periscope is a second-model sighting vane. This item is nothing more than a crude aiming device for the tank commander to point the main gun in the general direction of a target. When the gun was pointed in the direction of the target, the tank gunner's would hopefully see it through his turret-mounted periscope, which was fitted with a reticle for aiming and ranging. *Michael Green*

From a World War II Sherman tank manual comes this picture of the turret hydraulic traversing mechanism and all its various components. The Sherman turret could be traversed from the gunner's or the tank commander's position by both hydraulic or electric units. Because the Sherman's turret traversed faster than the turrets on German tanks, Sherman had a slight advantage in close-combat encounters.

Other Weapons

For dismounted use, the Sherman carried a metal tripod for mounting the vehicle's .30cal bow machine gun. Also carried was at least one Model 1928A1 Thompson sub-machine gun. The Tommy Gun was replaced in many US Shermans by the M3 sub-machine gun. A short, stubby, little weapon known as the Grease Gun, the M3 fired the same .45cal ammunition that the Thompson did. Its main advantage over the Thompson was that it was easy and cheap to make in wartime, much like the Sherman.

Sherman tanks also carried at least a dozen hand grenades for use by the crew when dismounted. An example of their use is described in the history of the 10th TB. One of its members, T. Sgt. Albert J. Schlichter, was awarded the Bronze Star for the following action:

"On September 3, 1944, at midnight, Sgt. Schlichter was a member of a tank crew on outpost duty in the Compiagne Forest in France. An enemy convoy trying to break through was stopped when the leading vehicle was knocked out. Sgt. Schlichter was assigned with Technical Four Miranda to watch and guard the right side of the road upon which the enemy vehicles were stretched out in a long line. During the entire night, enemy personnel, who had deserted their vehicles in the inception, attempted to regain their vehicles. They also kept up constant fire from the shelter of the woods.

"On several occasions, Sgt. Schlichter went out after the enemy with his personal weapon and hand grenades in order to keep them from getting back to their vehicles. This was a great personal risk as the enemy kept up constant small arms fire. Sgt. Schlichter personally captured four prisoners who were in a ditch by the road and who surrendered after he tossed a grenade in their direction. His actions materially aided in capturing ten vehicles, two 88mm guns, one 75mm gun, one antiaircraft gun, one 40mm gun, and 12 prisoners captured in addition to many killed. No members of his crew were hurt."

Some Sherman tankers went beyond using mere guns or grenades in their battles with the enemy. Pvt. Herbert H. Burr, assistant driver on a Sherman belonging to the 41st TB, 11th AD, won a Medal of Honor for his heroic acts near Dorrmoschel, Germany, on March 19, 1945. An enemy antitank rocket hit his tank, se-

While American tankers tended to favor the mounting of the .50cal machine gun on the turret of their Sherman tanks, some US Shermans mounted a .30cal machine gun, as pictured. The tank commander shown is speaking into a small hand-held microphone.

This close-up picture also presents an excellent view of the American military tankers crash helmet. This type of headgear offered no ballistic protection for the people who wore it. *US Army*

verely wounded the tank commander and forced the rest of the crew to abandon the vehicle. Burr, according to his military citations:

"Immediately climbed into the driver's seat and continued on the mission of entering the town to reconnoiter road conditions. As he rounded a turn, he encountered an 88mm antitank gun at point-blank range. Realizing that he had no crew, no one to man the tank's guns, he heroically chose to disregard his personal safety in a direct charge on the German weapon. At considerable speed, he headed straight for the loaded gun, which was fully manned by enemy troops who had only to pull the lanyard to send a shell into his vehicle. So unexpected and daring was his assault that he was able to drive his tank completely over the gun, demolishing it, and causing its crew to flee in confusion.

"He then skillfully sideswiped a large truck, overturned it, and wheeling his lumbering vehicle, returned to his company. When medical personnel who had been summoned to treat the wounded sergeant could not locate him, the valiant soldier ran through a hail of sniper fire to direct them to his stricken comrade. The bold, fearless determination of Private Burr, his skill and courageous devotion to duty, resulted in the completion of his mission in the face of seemingly impossible odds."

Although not talked about much, the Sherman tracks could be used to run over and crush enemy soldiers. On a number of occasions where dug-in enemy infantry refused to surrender and continued to fight, a Sherman track dropped into a slit trench and then "spun like crazy" took care of the occupants. General Bruce C. Clarke, a combat commander in the 4th AD and later the 7th AD said, "The track is in itself a major weapon system on the tank."

The sad part is in the confusion of combat, many American and Allied soldiers were also killed or maimed by their own tanks because they weren't seen or heard by the tank crews.

Chapter 6

Shermans in the Pacific

In the Pacific Island campaigns, the Sherman's fortunes were just the opposite of in Europe. In the Pacific, the Sherman with its 75mm cannon was Top Dog.

Compared to the Sherman, most Japanese tanks were obsolete in both firepower and armor protection. The most common Japanese tanks encountered by the Sherman during the war were the Type 95 Ha-Go light tank armed with a 37mm gun and two machine guns and the Type 97 medium tank armed with either a 37mm gun (in early versions) or a 47mm gun (in later production models). Known as the Shinhoto Chi-Ha, the Type 97 was also fitted with two machine guns.

Japanese tank tactics had been oriented offensively. The Japanese, who attempted to conquer all of China begin-

ning in the 1930s, used large numbers of tanks against masses of poorly armed Chinese troops and had been successful. These same offensive tactics when used against well-armed American military units equipped with Shermans and other weapons were not as productive.

The Marine Corps first used their M4A2s (diesel-powered) on Cape Gloucester, New Britain, in late December 1943. S/Sgt. Donald A. Hallman, Sr., a Marine combat correspondent describes the event.

"Marine Corps troops, using big General Sherman tanks to surprise an enemy which never expected to see the lumbering mediums in the middle of a jungle, knocked out 54 Jap pillboxes and 20 mountain howitzers in two days of fighting here.

"The General Shermans, taking direct hits from Jap 75mm's without faltering, cleared a path which forced the enemy to surrender a vital airport. More than 350 Japs were killed by shells from the medium American tanks. The Marine tank crews suffered only two dead but the Japs had inflicted other casualties on the Marines before the tanks could be brought up.

"Hitherto, the Japs had run into only

light tanks at Buna and Guadalcanal and the appearance of the General Shermans in the midst of the jungle morass that was the battlefield must have looked like an apparition to them.

"During the first day of the fighting, the Marines found four pillboxes holding up their advance on the airport. Marine engineers, using bulldozers to cut a path, built a road across the jungle swamp heavy enough to support the mediums. The tanks then cleared out the enemy entrenchments quickly.

"The second day the Japs tried to hold up the Marines advance with a series of 50 pillboxes and 20 mountain howitzers. The mediums went into action again and cleaned all of the pockets of resistance. Later, the bodies of more than 350 Japs were found buried in the blitzed entrenchments.

"The Japs, in defending the airport, counted on rivers, swamp and jungle to keep the Marines from advancing. However, they did not count on the Marine engineer and tank crews. The engineers, at one point, worked three days and nights without a stop to bridge 800 yards of swamp so tanks could be brought across.

"Light American tanks were used to

Japanese antitank guns took a toll on Sherman tanks during the war in the Pacific. A Japanese 47mm antitank gun has just hit these two M4A2 Sherman tanks, and they are already starting to burn. The Japanese 47mm gun firing a solid shot had a muzzle velocity of 2,700fps and could pierce a little over 2in of steel armor plate. *US Marine Corps*

Parked side by side are an M4A1 Sherman, armed with a 75mm gun, and a Japanese Army, World War II, Type 95 light tank armed with a 37mm cannon and two machine guns. The Type 95 was 14ft 4in long , 6ft 9in wide , and 7ft tall. It weighed 8–9 tons and had a top speed of 28mph. *Michael Green*

This Japanese Army Type 97 medium tank and its crew have been overwhelmed by superior American firepower. The Type 97 medium tank was armed with 37mm guns in early versions and 47mm guns in later production models. Having a crew of four, the Type 97 was powered by a diesel engine and weighed in at about 15 tons. *US Marine Corps*

clear out a valley of Jap resistance and the retreating enemy retired down a beach road where they set up their pill-boxes and blockades. It was then that the General Shermans did their slugging.

"The country definitely was not an area where light tanks much less the bigger mediums could be used. However, the Marine engineers flung up hasty bridges and roads to make the morass passable for the tanks."

In the Central Pacific campaigns, the Marines made extensive use of their Shermans in the taking of Japanese-held islands. In these battles, the Shermans' greatest problem sometimes seemed to be just getting from ship to shore.

In the battle for bloody Tarawa, the Marines used one company of M4A2s and two companies of M3A1s. The following extract from the book *War in the Pacific* (Office of the Chief of Military History, 1955) describes some of the problems the Shermans encountered.

"The platoon of medium tanks attached to the 3rd Battalion had been ordered by Major Schoettel to debark and the tanks were put into the water at the reef line, about 1,200 yards from dry land, while Company L was still struggling through the water toward shore. In front of them went the tank reconnaissance men to place guide flags in the potholes offshore.

"As soon as the guides entered the water, they were subjected to fierce fire from the enemy. Although the tanks came in safely in spite of this fire, most of the guides were killed or wounded. The vehicles came ashore on the left half of Red Beach 1, in the area swept most severely by Japanese fire. The sand was covered with the bodies of dead or wounded marines who could not yet be moved because of the intense fire. Rather than run the heavy tanks over these inert forms, the platoon commander decided to go back into the water, around to the extreme right flank of the beach, and then move inland from there. As the tanks executed this maneuver, four of them fell into potholes in the coral reef and were drowned out. Only two were able to make shore and these were shortly knocked out by 40mm gun fire."

On the Pacific island of Peleliu, which was invaded by Marine and Army units on September 15, 1944, seven Japanese light tanks supported by infantry attacked across an airfield against Marine

infantry supported by three M4A2s. In the ensuing battle, which the Marines had anticipated, most of the Japanese infantry were killed before they had a chance to reach the Marine lines. The Japanese light tanks that made it into the Marine positions were knocked out by the Shermans.

In the tank-versus-tank battle, the Marine M4A2s had to stop using M61 AP rounds because they passed right through the thin armor (1in or less) of the Japanese light tanks. Instead, the Marine tankers used the M48 HE rounds with instantaneous fuses. After the battle, the Marines found it hard to count exactly how many Japanese tanks had been used

Shown under a large camouflage net on Biak Island, New Guinea, April 10, 1944, the crew of this late-production M4 Sherman prepares for combat. The crewman on the left hands a Tommygun to the vehicle's driver. The crewman on the right is handing a 75mm round to the tank commander. *US Army*

in the attack. The M4's 75mm HE rounds had blown the Japanese tanks into unrecognizable bits and pieces.

Most Japanese tank units stationed on other Pacific islands knew that offensive

US Marine Corps M4A2 Sherman tanks first saw combat in the bloody battle for the small Pacific atoll of Tarawa in November 1943. This was the first time a landing by tanks was conducted on a beachhead under direct enemy fire. Because of their successful use on Tarawa, all Marine Corps tank units began getting rid of their M3 light tanks and replacing them with Shermans. Pictured on Tarawa is one of the few Sherman tanks to make it ashore during the battle. *US Marine Corps*

operations were useless against the Sherman. As a result, most Japanese tanks were dug-in as pillboxes. The major role for the Sherman became infantry support. The Sherman's 75mm gun was effective against all types of Japanese fortifications. From 1943 until the end of the war, the Sherman took part in almost every island-hopping campaign across the Pacific. While the number of Shermans used in

the Pacific was small when compared to the thousands upon thousands used in Europe, they still played an important role.

The last battle for the Marines and their Shermans occurred on the island of Okinawa which was within 350mi of the Japanese mainland. The battle started in April 1945 and lasted until June 1945, and was the biggest in the Pacific (almost 600,000 American military personnel took part). Maj. Gen. Lemuel C. Shepherd, Jr. (commander of the Marine 6th Division) praised the tank for its part in the battle. "If any one supporting arm can be singled out as having contributed more than any other during the progress of the campaign, the tank would be selected."

On the other side, Lt. Gen. Mitsuru Ushijima, commander of the Japanese 32nd Army of 100,000 men who defended Okinawa, stated in a dispatch to his

superiors in Tokyo that the "enemy's power lies in its tanks. It has become obvious that our general battle against the American forces is a battle against their tanks."

Both Marine Corps and US Army Shermans saw combat on Okinawa. The following extract from *War in the Pacific* describes the most deadly combat action seen by Shermans on Okinawa.

"At 0830, just before the infantry left the protection of the little fold in front of Kakazu, tanks in groups of three and four in column formation began moving across Kakazu Gorge; they then continued southward through the saddle between Kakazu and Nishibaru ridges. Altogether about 30 tanks, self-propelled assault guns, and armored flame-throwers moved out of the assembly area that morning for a power drive against the Japanese positions, Co. A of the 193rd TB making up that major part of the force.

This Marine tanker is probably trying to figure out how he is going to sneak the small Japanese light tank, fitted on the rear deck of the Sherman tank, home as a souvenir. Almost all World War II Marine tankers were trained at Jacques Farm, on Camp Elliot in Southern California. Operations training—which was divided into tactics, driving, gunnery, communications, and mapping—took about 12 weeks to finish. Maintenance training took only 8 weeks. *US Marine Corps*

Three tanks were lost to mines and road hazards in crossing the gorge and the saddle. As the tanks moved down the road in column, a 47mm antitank gun, firing from a covered position to the left on the edge of Nishibaru Ridge, destroyed four tanks with 16 shots, without receiving a single shot in return. The tank column hurried on south to look for a faint track leading into Kakazu that had shown on aerial photographs: the column

missed it, lost another tank to antitank fire, and then in error took a second little-used trail farther south and began working over enemy positions encountered in the face of the escarpment and in the relatively flat country to the east of Kakazu. Discovering that they could not reach the village from this point, the tanks retraced their way to the main road, turned back, found the right trail, and were in Kakazu shortly after 1000. They moved around and through the village, spreading fire and destruction; Kakazu was completely shot up and burned during the next three hours. Fourteen tanks were destroyed in and around the village, many by mines and 47mm antitank guns, others by suicide close-attack units, and more by artillery and mortar fire. During the six days, tanks in the Kakazu-Nishibaru area were destroyed by suicide attackers using 22-lb. satchel charges, which were usually thrown against the bottom plate. A majority of the tank crew members were still living after the tanks had been disabled,

but many were killed by enemy squads that forced the turret lids open and threw in grenades.

"At 1330, since it was now evident that infantry would not be able to reach them, the tanks received orders to return to their lines. Of the 30 tanks that had maneuvered around the left end of Kakazu Ridge in the morning, only eight returned in the afternoon. The loss of 22 tanks on 19 April in the Kakazu area was the greatest suffered by American armor on Okinawa in a single engagement. The tanks had operated wholly without infantry support. Four of the 22 were armored flamethrowers, and this was their first day in action. Some crew members of tanks destroyed by antitank gun fire dug pits under their tanks and remained hidden 40hr before they escaped, incredibly unmolested by the scores of Japanese within 100 yards.

"The Japanese had guessed that a tank-infantry attack would try to penetrate their lines between Nishibaru Ridge and Kakazu Ridge, and they had prepared carefully for it. Their plan was based on separating the infantry from the tanks. The 272nd Independent Infantry Battalion alone devised a fire net of four machine guns, two antiaircraft guns, three regimental guns, and the 81mm mortars of the 2nd Mortar Battalion to cover the saddle between the two ridges. The machine guns were sited at close range. In addition, two special squads of ten men each were sent forward to the saddle for close combat against the infantry. One group was almost entirely wiped out; the other had one noncommissioned officer wounded and three privates killed. The enemy defense also utilized the 47mm antitank guns of the 22nd Independent Antitank Gun Battalion and close-quarters suicide assault squads. So thorough were these preparations that the Japanese boasted, 'Not an infantryman got through.'"

By the end of the battle for Okinawa, over 147 Shermans had been destroyed. The design shortcomings of the Sherman and its lack of sufficient armor protection was becoming more appreciable as Japanese resistance stiffed. Had the American and Allied forces actually conducted an invasion of Japan, the losses among infantry and armored units equipped with Shermans could have been very high when faced with suicidal Japanese defensive measures.

Chapter 7

Improving the Sherman

As early as 1941, the Ordnance Branch of the US Army looked at equipping the Sherman with a larger gun.

76mm Cannon

To produce a new tank gun in the shortest amount of time possible, the Ordnance Branch used an existing 3in AP round as a starting point and built a new tank gun around it. Since the firing chamber of this new gun had to be long and slender to fit in the Sherman turret, the firing chamber was different from that of any other 3in gun then in service. But because difficulties would occur in the field if another 3in gun were introduced with a different size cartridge case, the Ordnance Branch decided to call this 3in gun a 76mm gun. The gun embodied the same physical characteristics as the 75mm gun but had a longer gun tube

Riding on the VVSS system, this M4A1 Sherman tank, armed with a 76mm gun, drives down a narrow country road near Odeigne, Belgium, on January 1, 1945. The 76mm gun had a muzzle velocity of 2,600fps with the M62 AP round. Unfortunately, this wasn't good enough to punch through the well-sloped armor of the Panther tank. *US Army*

which gave it a higher muzzle velocity and greater striking power than that attained with the 75mm gun.

Testing of the new gun began in August 1942. Results were so good that the gun was standardized and accepted into the Army inventory in September 1942, as the 76mm gun M1.

Despite the urging of Ordnance Branch officers, the Armored Board recommended in November 1942 that any quantity production of the new tank gun be deferred until it had more time to thoroughly test several pilot models and then be able to determine their tactical (battlefield) suitability.

The Armored Board was unhappy with what they believed was inadequate space in the existing Sherman turret for a 76mm gun. They were also unhappy with what they considered to be an unbalanced turret, even though the Ordnance Branch modified the existing Sherman turret with a bustle (rear turret) extension to better balance the new, heavier, and longer gun tube. The Armored Board decided it didn't want an improvised vehicle and ordered the entire project dropped.

The AGF (Army Ground Forces) felt that the trend of putting bigger guns on

tanks was incorrect. They believed that more effort should be directed to making the existing guns better. Normally, improving ammunition was the answer to make a tank gun more effective. The problem is that more powerful ammunition with higher muzzle velocity tends to create problems such as excessive erosion in gun tubes.

M4E6

Still plugging away, the Ordnance Branch began work in 1943 on the building of the two pilot vehicles of an improved Sherman design, known as the M4E6. Fitted with the preproduction turret and gun mount of a medium tank known as the T23 (roughly 200 of which were built), the M4E6 turret was fitted with an improved 76mm M1 gun known as the 76mm M1A1 gun. Built by Chrysler, the two M4E6 pilot vehicles performed well during firing tests. The Army was pleased since the new turret also offered more room for the crew.

Unlike what happened in 1942, the AGF decided in 1943 that they wanted 1,000 of the new M4E6 tanks armed with the 76mm gun to be built as soon as possible. They also decided to discontinue building the 75mm gun.

The difference between November 1942 and August 1943 was that in early 1943, the Army had finally decided that they would probably fight the rest of the war with the Sherman and that they better improve its combat efficiency as soon as possible. The M4E6 tank was one answer to that problem.

While the AGF wanted 1,000 of the new M4E6s with the 76mm gun, the Armored Board did not want to completely stop production of the 75mm gun. They knew from combat reports that the HE ammunition for the 75mm gun was better than that for the 76mm gun. The Army also thought that the muzzle blast from the 76mm raised too much smoke and dust and hindered a tank crew from aiming its gun a second or third shot.

Using a new long-primer ammunition and installing a muzzle brake on the 76mm gun of the M4E6 Sherman re-

duced the problem of target obstruction. With the fitting of a muzzle brake, the 76mm M1A1 was redesignated as the M1A1C. An even later model of the 76mm gun with a different rifling was known as the M1A2.

A muzzle brake is a device fitted to the muzzle of a gun that deflects the discharge gases rearward through ports. This results in a force applied to the brake in a direction opposite to the recoil. To keep down the amount of dust kicked up by the muzzle blast from a gun, the ports are usually located in the sides of the brake.

Maj. Paul A. Bane, Jr., from the 3rd TB, 67th AR, stated in a report:

Shown at Aberdeen Proving Ground in July 1943 is this early pilot model of the M4E6 Sherman medium tank. The M4E6 was used to test the possibility of mounting a 76mm gun into the turret of a prototype tank (known as the T20 series), then mating the new gun-armed turret into a standard Sherman tank hull. The hull of the vehicle pictured is an interesting example of the least-common Sherman tank hull, the composite model. This mated the ballistically superior shaped front hull plate of the cast-hull Sherman tank with the roomier three-fourths rear section of the welded-hull Sherman tank. *US Army*

The business end of the 76mm gun mounted on an M4A3 Sherman tank. This particular vehicle is from an early production run, as it still has the VVSS system. *US Army*

In the middle of a flock of sheep, this M4A3 Sherman tank armed with a 76mm gun has the older VVSS system. The 76mm gun is in the hull-mounted travel lock. The travel lock protects the tank's main gun from unnecessary movement when not in a combat environment. Most Allied tankers considered the Sherman tank with the 76mm gun somewhat top heavy. For Allied tankers fighting in the very mountainous terrain of Italy, on narrow country roads, a top-heavy tank was a definitive concern. *US Army*

Tankers of the 761st Tank Battalion, US Army, crewed this M4A1 Sherman tank armed with a 76mm gun. The photo was taken on November 11, 1944, near Nancy, France. The vehicle has its main gun in the travel lock. While all Sherman tank models weighed less than the German Panthers or Tigers, the German tanks, due to their better design, had better cross-country mobility than did the Shermans. *US Army*

"Our tank crews operating tanks equipped with 76mm guns have experienced great difficulty observing the strike of a round due to excessive muzzle blast. It was necessary to use dismounted observers. Recently we have received a few M4A3E8 tanks equipped with muzzle brakes. Test firing and combat operations have proven the muzzle brake to be a great help. We consider muzzle brakes

an essential part of the tank gun."

The 76mm gun mounted in the M4E6 tank fired an AP round known as the M62 APC (armored piercing capped). Later versions of this round were fitted with an HE filler using a base detonating fuse designed to explode within the target. The M62 APC round fired from the 76mm gun had a muzzle velocity of 2,600fps compared to the 2,030fps of the 75mm gun.

In the field, the M62 APC round fired from a 76mm gun proved to be a disappointment. 2nd Lt. Frank Seydel, Jr., describes a combat action in which M62 APC round was used.

"On March 3rd at Bosinghoven, I took under fire two German Mark V Panther tanks at a range of 600 yards. At this time, I was using a 76mm gun, using APC for my first round. I saw this round make a direct hit on a vehicle and ricochet into the air. I fired again at a range of 500 yards and again observed a direct hit, after which I threw about 10 rounds of mixed APC and HE, leaving the German tank burning."

Early in 1943 the US Army expressed its confidence in the first generation of Sherman tanks (M4, M4A1, M4A2, M4A3). At the same time, they requested that numerous modifications be made to improve the Sherman combat efficiency and include additional provisions for crew safety.

The manufacturers could make some of these modifications with little production difficulty. Others, however, involved a considerable amount of research and design time, making it necessary to postpone them until they could be worked out properly and until they could be applied without causing any delays in production rates.

During March, April, and May 1943, Aberdeen Proving Ground worked on a number of modifications to M4A1 Shermans, and submitted a detailed report suggesting many changes. At about this same time, three M4A1s, Shermans repre-

new vehicles; the M4 series terminology was continued, with new model designations added. The M4A1 became the M4A1 (76mm) Gun, Wet. The M4A2 became the M4A2 (76mm) Gun, Wet. The M4A3 became the M4A3 (76mm) Gun, Wet.

Upon standardization of the second-generation M4 series tanks with the 76mm gun and the wet ammunition racks, the production of vehicles with the 75mm gun was limited to tanks with the Ford V–8 GAA engine. This vehicle, which also had wet ammunition racks and other improvements, was designated as the M4A3 (75mm) Gun, Wet.

The first generation of Shermans (M4, M4A4, and M4A6) were never upgraded with a 76mm gun. They retained their original 75mm guns until their production ceased. A large number of early first-generation M4 models and an even larger number of M4A3 models were converted or built to carry a turret-mounted 105mm howitzer.

Wet Ammunition Stowage

Combat experience with first-generation Sherman tanks armed with the 75mm gun showed that 60–90 percent of them were destroyed by burning and almost all of them burned when hit by a German Panzerfaust. Most Sherman fires originated in their ammunition racks. A few slow fires began in the oil in the powertrain or the stowage or engine compartment. Experience of the 9th Army's second-generation Shermans with wet stowage showed that only 5–10 percent of their 76mm Shermans burned. Records of the 1st Army showed no difference.

Opinion at the time held that wet stowage delayed the initial rate of fire, and that more than one hit was required to start a serious fire. The Army practice of loading extra ammunition in the Sherman turret and its unprotected ready racks made a scientific evaluation of any benefits from wet stowage impossible.

senting three stages of modification, were furnished to the Armored Board for tests, and most of the suggested changes were reported on favorably.

By autumn of 1943, however, the number of changes required for the Armored Board had so increased that it was considered advisable to effect a major redesign of the Sherman series, which might also apply to the vehicle with the 76mm gun being developed by the Ordnance Branch.

Chrysler was authorized to build pilot models incorporating the numerous requested changes. These models were to include the latest manufacturing modifications and serve as pilots in checking releases. In addition to the new turrets and mounts for the 76mm gun, other major modifications were contemplated: 1) incorporation of a vision cupola; 2) provision for stowage of ammunition in the

lower hull to reduce the fire hazard; 3) use of a new front plate with larger doors for the driver and assistant driver; 4) provision for water-protected ammunition racks in the 75mm and 76mm gun armed M4 series (vehicles so equipped would have the designation W added, and the water would contain ethylene glycol to prevent freezing and a rust inhibitor known as Ammudamp); 5) changes in the electrical system; 6) improvements in the driver's controls, to reduce driving effort; and 7) improvements in installation of components in the engine compartment, including winterization equipment, improved fuel systems to eliminate vapor lock, and improved clutch linings.

Subsequently, these and other changes were authorized for production. The tanks incorporating these changes were so different from earlier vehicles that they justified being regarded as three

Because of the greater width of the HVSS tracks, a running board was placed on each side of the hull of vehicles so equipped, as shown on this Easy Eight. The vehicle pictured belongs to the US Army 15th Tank Company. The location is near Duino, Italy, on January 15, 1948. *US Army*

With the change to liquid-protected ammunition stowage, a partial basket, which occupied only about one-third of the space, replaced the full turret basket. The partial basket permitted access to the ammunition stowed under the sub-floor as well as the material stowed around the space available. It also increased accessibility to the driving compartment and thus added an important safety factor. Later changes eliminated the basket completely, and the seats were supported by

brackets hanging from the ledge of the turret.

Improved Electrical System

Electrical equipment was removed from the hull floor and concentrated in the left upper hull, thus simplifying the installation of these units and making them more accessible. The wiring system was revised to make wiring harness in the various tanks as nearly universal as possible. The auxiliary engine exhaust was enclosed in a duct, which also included an electric heating coil energized from the auxiliary generator, permitting application of heat to the battery box or to the engine compartment as required. Voltage regulators, instruments, switches, and other components were sealed against dust and moisture. The tachometer was removed from the engine and located on the rear of the transmission and belt-driven from the propeller shaft.

Engine Compartment Improvements

The various components in the engine compartment were relocated for greater efficiency and accessibility. Provision was made for installation of winterization equipment. A gasoline heater and the necessary inlet and outlet air shutters were made available in kits.

New Clutch

The Lipe 16in two-plate clutch, as used on the early M4s and M4A1s was "one of the major weaknesses of the vehicle," according to a January 1944 letter from Aberdeen Proving Grounds. It was criticized for excessive drag caused by incomplete disengagement, high pedal pressure, need for frequent adjustment, and recurring mechanical failures. The Borg and Beck 17.5in clutch was devel-

This M4E8 Sherman belongs to the Patton Museum at Fort Knox, Kentucky, and is shown being put through its paces with some of the museum's other historical vehicles.
Richard Bryd

oped and proved superior to the previous clutch. In April 1944, the Ordnance Committee noted that the Borg and Beck 17.5in clutch was being released for production on Shermans using Continental R-975-C1 or -C4 engines. The committee directed that all requisitions for complete assemblies overseas should be filled by shipment of the Borg and Beck clutch as soon as available, whereas domestic requisitions would be filled by supplying the Lipe clutch until stocks were exhausted.

New Commander's Cupola

In response to an insistent demand for improved vision for Sherman commanders, the Libby-Owens-Ford Glass Co. developed a new vision cupola. The new cupola was fitted with six laminated glass vision blocks uniformly spaced around a central 21in diameter hatch. The six vision blocks gave Sherman commanders a 360deg field of view. There was also a periscope installed in a rotating mount in the central hatch cover. In actual combat, Sherman tank commanders tended to stick their heads out of the turret to have a better view of what was happening around their vehicles. This was a dangerous practice, but as one American tanker put it, "I wanted to hear which way the bullets were coming from." German tank commanders did the same and also suffered losses for it.

Horizontal Volute Spring Suspension

The suspension system used on the early M4 tanks employed the VVSS (Vertical Volute Spring Suspension) system and 16 9/16in track. This was the result of several projects for improved suspensions. In September 1943, the Ordnance Committee recommended developing Horizontal Volute Spring Suspension (HVSS) systems and 23in center-guided tracks for application to pilot vehicles, designated M4E8. Tests proved this suspension superior to the VVSS system in durability, flotation, riding qualities, and road wheel life.

As the name indicates, this volute spring was placed horizontally instead of vertically. Elimination of friction from sliding shoes, improved geometric design, addition of shock absorbers, and rubber-tired idlers made for a smoother ride and, together with the use of center-guides instead of outside guides, decreased the possibility of track-throwing. The wide track required the use of dual

bogies, doubling the number of bogie wheels and distributing the wear more uniformly.

In February 1944, procurement was authorized for 500 76mm M4A3s with wet ammunition stowage. In March 1944, the Ordnance Committee recommended HVSS on all new Shermans.

These changes increased the weight of the new Shermans by about 5,000lb and increased the width over sand shields from 105in to 117.75in. On the positive side, the increased width of the new tracks reduced ground pressure from 14.5lb/sq-in to 11.0lb/sq-in. Because of the greater width of the vehicle with the 23in tracks, a running board was placed at each side, from which the sand shields were hung, instead of from the upper hull. In February 1945, the Ordnance Committee authorized the omission of sand shields from new production Shermans.

Fielding the 76mm Sherman

The Army decided that it couldn't wait for all the new improvements to be incorporated into the second-generation Sherman. So even before the completion of the prototypes, the Army pressed the builders to start production of the 76mm Sherman. The Pressed Steel Car Co. managed to produce the first 100 76mm M4A1s in January 1944, the first of over 3,400 built. The Fisher Co., builders of the M4A2 diesel engine Sherman, began production of 76mm versions in May 1944. The M4A3, the most preferred in the US Army and its ultimate production model, was first built with the 76mm gun in March 1944 by Chrysler. Chrysler was also still building at the time a modernized second-generation Sherman with a 75mm gun and a wet stowage system.

M4A3E8 Easy Eight

By August 1944, Chrysler had switched from building 76mm M4A3 tanks fitted with the older, first-generation VVSS system to the new and improved second-generation HVSS system. These new production M4A3s, which featured all the second-generation modifications, were designated as the M4A3 (76mm, Wet), HVSS. Among American soldiers, this particular version of the Sherman was popularly known as the Easy Eight. The tank acquired this nickname during its test phase when it was known as the M4A3E8.

The Easy Eight was built by Chrysler up until April 1945, with a total of 2,617 produced. Fisher also built 525 Easy Eights before the end of the war, bringing the total production figure to 3,142.

Only a small number of early M4A1 (76mm), Wet, Shermans came off the production lines in time to be shipped off to England for D-day. While the buildup of troops and equipment in England for the invasion of Europe was in full gear, a number of demonstrations of the new 76mm Sherman were arranged. Everyone who saw the demonstrations was impressed. Yet most armor commanders decided that they would rather stick with the familiar 75mm gun than retrain their troops to use a new gun. Even General Patton who witnessed a demonstration of the 76mm gun on June 12, 1944, decided he would take the new gun into use if they were first placed into separate tank battalions for a combat test.

This lack of interest in a bigger and supposedly better gun for the Sherman seems strange for those who look back in hindsight. At the time, though, the US Army and its commanders still had complete faith in the 75mm Shermans. Combat in North Africa and fighting in Sicily and Italy had shown that the Sherman compared well with older model German tanks of the time. While a small number of German Tiger I tanks saw action in both North Africa and later in Italy, poor tactics and even worse terrain limited their effectiveness, giving American tankers a false sense of security. The German Panther tank saw limited action in Italy, but also failed to generate any doubts in the ability of the 75mm gun armed Sherman to do its job.

The 76mm Sherman in Combat

By June 10, 1944, Hitler's Atlantic Wall had crumbled. While there had been a few early moments during the invasion that had been touch and go for the Allied invasion forces, they soon held an 80mi stretch of the Normandy coast.

For the 75mm Shermans, the first hint of real trouble began in the southern Normandy countryside. There, dense and heavy hedges that were centuries old crossed local farmer's fields. These hedges grew out of earthen banks 3–4ft high. Many times these hedges were double rows forming a large but narrow trench between them.

In these narrow hedgerows, the US Sherman tankers first ran into the Panther tank. The Sherman's 75mm gun proved almost completely useless against the German tanks' thick, well-sloped armor hide. Even the Army's senior commanders were now aware that their faith in the Sherman's 75mm gun was misplaced. When this news got to Gen. Dwight Eisenhower (Supreme Allied Commander), he was quoted in Gen. Omar Bradley's autobiography, *A Soldier's Story,* to have said:

"You mean our 76 won't knock these Panthers out? I thought it was going to be the wonder gun of the war.

"Why is it that I am always the last to hear about this stuff? Ordnance told me this 76 would take care of anything the Germans had. Now I find you can't knock out a damn thing with it."

The 76mm gun's inability to punch through the frontal armor of German tanks can be blamed squarely on the Ordnance Department. It was their failure to correctly assess the technical capabilities of German armor plate that led to the deployment of weapons like the 76mm gun that could not fulfill the roles intended for it.

The Ordnance Department had been provided with information on both the Tiger and Panther, yet they completely failed to properly evaluate it. The end result was that American tank guns and their penetration ability of enemy armor plate were overestimated and the quality of German armor plate and the way it was designed discounted.

As an example, throughout the war, the Ordnance Department tested the effectiveness of its guns and ammunition against nearly vertical plates of steel armor which did not match that of any German tank. While the Ordnance Department did try to account for the increased effectiveness of sloping armor plate by using mathematical calculations, they failed to take into account the tendency of tank rounds to bounce (or ricochet) off from angled armor plate.

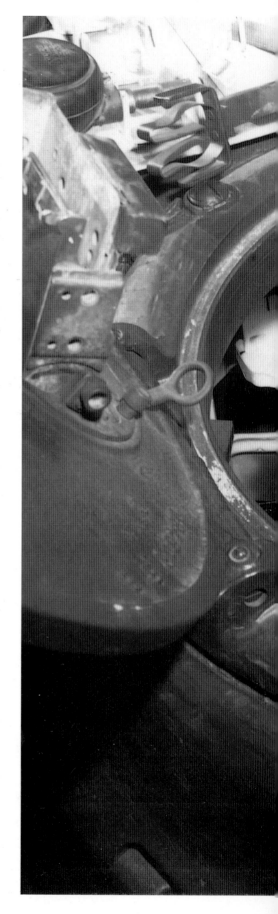

Looking down the loader's hatch of an Easy Eight, the loader and the breech end of the 76mm gun are visible. Behind the loader's head is the mounting bracket for the coaxial .30cal machine gun. Unlike most Shermans, some models of the 76mm-armed Shermans had a large circular hatch for the loader, as pictured. *US Army*

391988

This photo shows the many visible differences between a first-generation M4 Sherman tank with a 75mm gun and narrow VVSS system and a second-generation M4A1 cast-hull Sherman tank armed with a 76mm gun and fitted with the wider HVSS system. *Michael Green*

In September 1943, Maj. Gen. Alvan C. Gillem (Armored Force commander) wrote a letter to Gen. Lesley J. McNair (AGF commander) stating that, based on figures by the Ordnance Department, the 76mm gun could penetrate the frontal armor of the Tiger tank at a range of 2,000yd. This figure proved to be incredibly optimistic since combat in Europe (1944) showed that the 76mm gun could only penetrate the Tiger's frontal armor at less than 50yd.

The Ordnance Department's optimistic assessment of American tank guns was so convincing to itself and the rest of the Army that, up until American tanks battled the German tanks in Normandy, it

was almost impossible for the Ordnance Department to get any tank destroyers with bigger guns into production. Once American tankers discovered how under-gunned the Sherman was in combat, it was just the opposite. With soldiers at all levels from bottom to the top screaming for tanks with bigger guns, General Eisenhower sent his own personnel staff Armored Force officer to the United States to help expedite the development and production of a 90mm gun and heavy tank. What was not said was that this same officer had been given the embarrassing task of reopening a project he had been instrumental in canceling.

Unfortunately, by July 1944, there was no possible way for American know-how to produce a better class of tank gun before the end of the war. If the US Army had foreseen the problem in 1943, rather than 1944, tank designers and factories might have been able to produce an up-gunned Sherman that could have effectively dealt with the Panther or Tiger I or

II. Sgt. Nick Moceri in a wartime report stated:

"I've been told that the M4A3 tank (with 76mm gun) is the equal if not a better tank than the German Mark V Panther. That's not so! The only reason that we've gone as far as we have is summed up in 'Quantity and the Cooperation of Arms.' Until such time as the army puts out a tank gun that can knock out a Panther from the front at 1500 yards, or adds enough armor to stop a shell from the same distance, we'll continue to lose a heavy toll of tanks, men and equipment."

Sgt. Francis W. Baker, a tank commander, stated in the same report:

"On the morning of November 20, 1944, I was tank commander of a Sherman mounting a 76mm gun. The Germans staged a counterattack with infantry supported by at least three Mark V tanks. Ordering my gunner to fire at the closest tank, which was approximately 800 yards away, he placed one right in the side which was completely visible to me. To

The crew of this Easy Eight Sherman has welded an Army-supplied, add-on armor kit to the front of their vehicle. The add-on armor extends all the way down to the cast front-mounted transmission housing. The vehicle itself is armed with a 76mm gun and has HVSS. The crew of this vehicle have also mounted an extra .30cal machine gun on the top of the turret for added firepower.
US Army

my amazement and disgust I watched the shell bounce off the side. My gunner fired at least six more rounds at the vehicle hitting it from the turret to the track. This German tank, knowing that I possibly would be supported by a tank destroyer, started to pull away. I was completely surprised to see it moving after receiving seven hits from my gun. At this time a tank destroyer mounting a 90mm gun pulled up to my right flank, motioning to the commander, he acknowledged that he saw the tank. With one well placed shot he put it in flames. Traversing to his

left he also put another one in flames."

Cpl. George C. Miller also stated in the same report:

"On 17 November 1944 in the vicinity of Puffendorf, Germany, fired 76mm APC at a German Mark V tank. The range was 800 yards. The return fire from this enemy tank hit the right final drive, penetrating through the final drive, stopping in the turret. This Mark V tank manned a 75mm gun.

"Consider the 76mm gun improperly balanced. Re-laying is necessary after every round is fired. A variation of 100 to 200 yards results when fired at a range of 1000 yards or more."

Improved Tank Ammunition

In order to further increase the penetrating ability of the 76mm gun, the Army gave high priority to a project for developing a special shell for the 76mm gun, which would increase its penetration ability. The round was based on the use of a tungsten-carbide core, using an alu-

minum outer wall to surround the tungsten carbide. This round gave increased penetration and was known as the 76mm high-velocity armor-piercing (HVAP) round. As soon as these rounds were manufactured, they were transported by air to Europe and then to the tankers in the field. Thus each 76mm gun armed Sherman tank in Europe was supposed to have a moderate supply of this special ammunition.

Maj. Paul A. Bane, Jr., from the 3rd TB, 67th AR, stated in a report:

"Our tank crews have had some success with the HVAP 76mm ammunition. However, at no time have we been able to secure more than five rounds per tank and in recent actions this has been reduced to a maximum of two rounds, and in many tanks all this type has been expended without being replaced."

An April 27, 1945, letter to the Office of the Army's Surgeon General from Col. Willard Machle and Lt. Gen. Frederick S. Brackett, who went to observe problems

in tank units in Europe, stated:

"The 76mm gun is well liked for use against light armor, but universally the demand is for a great increase in velocity of the full might projectile even though the life of gun is reduced to as little as 200 rounds (400 considered desirable). HVAP has not been available in sufficient quantity to have any significant influence. Tankers' grab for it as a drowning man a straw, though few regard it as adequate. The universal demand is that our gun be basically at least as good as the German 75 Kwk 42. Our HVAP would then play the role of the German AP40 shot. The muzzle brake is universally demanded."

1st Lt. James A. White of the 67th AR, whose unit was using both 75mm and 76mm M4s, stated in a report:

"I believe the M4A3E8 tank with the 76mm gun and muzzle brake is the best tank and gun that I have seen, and will be very successful if we obtain enough high-velocity AP ammunition."

Capt. Charles B. Kelley of Co. D, 66th AR, stated in a report:

"There is a general conviction that all 76mm guns should have more HVAP ammunition available. At present this type of ammunition is extremely limited. Experience and tests have shown this to be superior to the APC ammunition. All available HVAP ammunition should be issued and put to immediate use, rather than stored in dumps."

Sgt. Ross Figueroa of the 2nd AD

stated in a report:

"The facts have been proven to me and my gunner on more than one occasion. We in E Company have been trying for a long time to get more of the HVAP ammunition. We have found that the HVAP does not bounce off the enemy tanks like the APC.

"The last incident happened on March 2nd, when I gave my gunner the order to fire at an enemy Mark V tank at the range of 1600 yards with first round which was APC and it bounced off. My second round was HVAP which destroyed the Mark V and set it on fire."

Figueroa went on in his report to describe another combat action in Germany:

"While on the right of the village of Fischeln, Germany, I was placed in a firing position by the platoon leader. In my position I had a field of fire extending to a distance of 2000 yards, covering several roads. While in this position, I spotted a Mark V moving across my front. For my first shot I used an APC, establishing my range, which was 1600 yards. The next round was an HVAP. It hit the tank, immediately setting it on fire.

"Later I had an opportunity to inspect the tank and upon seeing the size of the hole made by the projectile I am confident in the shell and would like to have more of the ammunition. With such ammunition I wouldn't be afraid to shoot at any of the enemy vehicles, especially at

ranges where our normal ammunition now ricochets off of the enemy armor.

"I honestly believe that we should have much more of the ammo than is now being issued. The few rounds (4) we now have are hardly sufficient, should we ever encounter enemy armor in numbers. The HVAP ammo has proved beyond a doubt its value, especially when I know it will penetrate enemy armor at 1600 yards or more.

"I feel that we should have more of the high-velocity ammo and if possible half of our basic load should be of that type."

The HVAP round was good, but it did not always do the job. 1st Lt. William L. Schaubel described in a wartime report a combat encounter with Tigers in which he used HVAP.

"At Oberemot, Germany, 27 February 1945, our second platoon on road block was engaged by 2 Tiger tanks, Mark VI, at 3,600 yards, and two of our Shermans were knocked out. Our 3,400 feet per second 76mm HVAP ammunition was used and bounced off the side slopes, seven rounds. Definitely outranged due to better sights in the Mark VI and more muzzle velocity in their suped up ammunition. Upon throwing smoke at the Tiger tanks, they withdrew because smoke means marking target for artillery and fighter-bombers to the Germans."

90mm Shermans

The most unfortunate aspect of the Sherman upgunning process is that the Army had a chance to mount a 90mm-gun-armed turret on the Sherman in 1943.

The Office of the Chief of Military History, in their published work on the technical services in World War II, talked about the aborted development of a 90mm Sherman.

Massed at Eelde Airport, Holland, on May 23, 1945, is the 5th Canadian Armored Division. Pictured side by side are Shermans equipped with both the British 17-pounder and the shorter American-built 75mm guns.
Canadian Army

"An attempt by the Armored Force Board in the fall of 1943 to provide the M4 with a more powerful gun, the 90mm, had failed. Ordnance had begun development work on the 90mm antiaircraft gun to adapt it for use on tanks and gun motor carriages early in the war, after reports from Cairo had indicated that the Germans in Libya were successfully using their 88mm gun against tanks, and the new antitank 90mm was standardized as the M3 in September 1943. Thereupon, the Armored Force Board, believing that the M4 Sherman tank was the one tank that could be delivered in time for the invasion of Europe, recommended that the 90mm gun be installed on a thousand M4A3 tanks. Maj. Gen. Gladeon M. Barnes, chief of the Ordnance Department's Research and Development Service, refused to go along with the recommendation; and General McNair turned it down on the advice of his G-3 Brig. Gen. John M. Lentz."

Barnes had nothing against the 90mm gun; on the contrary, he and Col. Joseph M. Colby, chief of the Development and Engineering Department at the Ordnance Tank-Automotive Center in Detroit, had done everything they could to get it to the battlefield on a tank destroyer, over the determined opposition of AGF, whose New Developments Division continued to insist that 75mm and 76mm guns were adequate. Thanks largely to Barnes' efforts, backed up by the Tank Destroyer Board, the M36 self-propelled 90mm got to Europe in time to play its part in the Roer plain battles. But Barnes did not want the 90mm on the Sherman tank. He believed the gun was too heavy for the tank; that it produced "too much of an unbalanced design."

After the Allied invasion of Europe, the Army quickly became aware of the limitations of the 76mm gun firing its standard AP ammunition. Gen. Omar Bradley noted that the 76mm gun often "scuffed rather than penetrated" the heavy armor of the Panthers and Tigers.

In July 1944, General Eisenhower sent Gen. Joseph A. Holly (his staff armored officer) back to the United States

to urge the shipment to Europe of more M36 tank destroyers mounting the 90mm gun. While in Detroit, Holly, by chance, was shown an M4 Sherman modified by Chrysler to carry a 90mm gun. While he thought it had "tempting possibilities," he quickly was convinced by the Ordnance Department that it would be better to wait for the fielding of the T26E1 tank, already mounting a 90mm gun (this vehicle eventually became the M26 Pershing tank), which would be available before the end of 1944. Unfortunately, the fielding of the T26E1 was delayed to the end of the war.

Many American tankers tended to believe that no matter what the Ordnance Department did, the M26 Pershing tank would never have made it to Europe in time to be of any real value during the war. Instead, many believed that had the Sherman been modified to mount a 90mm gun in 1943 (if only as a backup for the M26 Pershing's failure to get into combat in late 1944), it would have provided enough firepower in Europe to save the lives of many Sherman tankers who were killed or wounded due to their vehicles being so undergunned.

Firefly Shermans

The British Army, like the US Army, began early in 1941 to think about putting bigger, more powerful tank guns in their vehicles. But it wasn't until 1943, with the Panther's appearance in Italy and reports from the Soviet Army about their own tank battles with newer and heavier German tanks, that the British be-

gan to really think about mounting their 76.2mm towed antitank gun into the turret of a tank.

The British military sometimes used the old traditional method of naming a cannon according to the weight of its projectile rather than the size of its bore. As a result, their 76.2mm gun, which fired a round that weighed 17 British pounds, became a 17-pounder. The 17-pounder gun lacked HE ammunition until the end of the war, but its AP round was far superior to the standard American designed 76mm gun ammunition.

Originally, the British planned to mount their 17-pounder on one of their own tank designs, but nothing worked right. Because of the large number of Shermans available, the British decided to fit their 17-pounder into the tank. The British, like the Americans, found that their gun was somewhat cramped in a turret it wasn't designed for. To make it fit correctly, the British designed a new mount and recoil system for the 17-pounder. To make more room in the turret, the British moved the vehicle's radio set into an armored box welded to the rear of the turret.

There were two different types of 17-pounder guns fitted into the Sherman turret. Almost identical, they were both fitted with a lightweight double baffle muzzle brake and a semiautomatic horizontal sliding breechblock.

Wisely, the British decided to start production of this new vehicle, nicknamed the Firefly, as soon as possible, with the result that by D-day the British

The crew of this Canadian Army Sherman Firefly have covered the barrel of their gun with brushwood to camouflage its long, distinctive shape from enemy antitank gunners. *Canadian Army*

Army had at least one Firefly in each of its tank troops (four tanks). The official designation for the vehicle was the Sherman VC.

The 17-pounder gun fitted in the Sherman turret was roughly equivalent to the German Panther tank's 75mm gun. It was also slightly superior in penetration of armor plate to both early model German 88mm guns like that found on the Tiger I and the 90mm tank gun as found in the US Army's M36 tank destroyer and M26 Pershing tank.

To make more room for ammunition, the British Army took out the assistant driver and his bow machine gun position. Reducing the crew to four allowed the Firefly to carry up to 78 rounds of 17-pounder ammunition. Fourteen of these rounds were carried where the assistant driver's position used to be. The rest of the tank rounds were divided between five ready rounds in two bins on the turret basket floor and the rest in three bins under the turret floor.

The Firefly's 17-pounder gun fired an AP round known as armor-piercing capped ballistic capped (APCBC) solid shot. Two months later, another round known as super-velocity discarding sabot (SVDS) was introduced into service. (The SVDS was also referred to as armor-piercing discarding sabot or APDS.) Much like the US Army HVAP round, this ammunition consisted of a high-density tungsten-carbide core in a lightweight carrier. The projectile weighed 7.91lb, of which 5.5lb was the core. The lightweight carrier surrounding the core pushed the round out of the 17-pounder tank barrel at higher muzzle velocity (3,950fps) and then separated from the core after leaving the muzzle. This reduced drag, allowing the projectile to retain its high velocity to a greater range.

Because the British Firefly was one of the only Allied tanks at the beginning of the invasion of Europe that posed a serious threat to German tanks like the Panther and Tiger, it quickly became a priority target for German tankers. Since the long barrel of the 17-pounder gun was the tank's most easily identified visual feature, some British tank crews tried to find ways to camouflage the barrel. One method involved the fitting of a metal can a little over halfway to the end of the bar-

rel, and then painting the forward half of the barrel with a pattern that would break up its outline, hopefully giving it the impression of a shorter, 75mm gun.

Firefly in Action

Reprinted with permission of *AFV News* and its editor George Bradford, is the following excerpt of an interview by Doug Devin with Capt. Dan Beggs, a former Firefly gunner in the Canadian 1st Hussars.

"'I think the 17-pounder was every bit as powerful as the 88. We had a fighting chance with that gun.' [Beggs] says the tactics usually used were to let the 75mm armed Shermans go forward with the Fireflies hanging back a bit. That way, if the opposition turned out to be the thinner-skinned vehicles such as the Mark IVs, the 75mms could take care of them. 'We (Fireflies) didn't bother with the Mark IVs.'

"However, in the event of heavier metal showing up in the form of Konigstigers [Tiger II], then the Fireflies were in a position to stalk the monsters, looking for that key flank shot. If necessary to shoot it out with Tiger IIs from the front, Capt. Beggs says that the only thing to do was try and get a round into the shot trap under the mantel. Like all Allied tankers, he preferred not to see the Tiger II from the front. It was usually possible to outmaneuver them due to their limited numbers and sluggish nature. 'That Tiger Royal was their best, but like all German tanks the turret traverse was too slow. It was their downfall.'

"Capt. Beggs knows of what he speaks, for no less than five Tiger IIs fell prey to his gunnery. Mind you, things went both ways. 'I've got five Tiger Royals to my credit and they've got one of me. One day there was a hell of a bang from the side of the turret and something passes just in front of my face and went right out the other side!' Capt. Beggs claims that he emerged from that incident with singed eyebrows, but he may have been pulling my leg. But I certainly don't doubt his statement that having an 88 round pass through both sides of the turret caused the crew's confidence in the Sherman's armor to decline.

"Capt. Beggs doesn't count another later run-in with the 88 as really being

Destroyed during the fierce fighting around the French city of Caen in 1944, this Tiger II shows both the well-sloped armor and powerful 88mm cannon that made it such a threat to Allied tanks like the Sherman. Designed to replace the Tiger I, only 485 Tiger II tanks were built by the Germans before the war ended. *British Tank Museum*

knocked out, since the damage was able to be repaired in the field. 'I can remember seeing the grass parting towards us, then I felt a sudden bump across the front of the tank and the driver shouted that he couldn't steer anymore.' Realizing that they were a sitting duck for a Tiger they couldn't even see, the crew wisely decided to join their brethren in the poor-bloody-infantry for awhile. When the area had been cleared, they returned to recover their tank. Once again they had been lucky, the 88 round had hit the nose of the Sherman in just such a way that it had glanced downward, gone through

the transmission and exited out the belly. Being shot at from such extreme ranges wasn't unusual. 'Those 88's were deadly accurate even out to 3000 yards. We hardly ever engaged at greater than 800 yards, 1000 yards at the very most.'

"All things considered though, he says the Sherman was 'a most efficient tank.' He also heartily agrees with the view that Allied air power was of paramount importance in defeating the high-quality German forces. 'Those German panzer units were good. You had to be sharp and fast when they were around. As for the SS, whatever else you can say about them, when they were going, they were going ahead. Our air superiority was decisive. We would have taken a shellacing a few times without it.'"

The British did offer the design of the 17-pounder in the Sherman turret to the US Army, but prior to the invasion of Europe the Army and its commanders had no interest at all, other than to criticize it!

After D-day, Gen. Omar Bradley asked British General Field-Marshall Sir Bernard Montgomery if one Sherman in each American tank platoon could be fitted with a 17-pounder gun. Unfortunately by this time, the British Army wanted every Firefly with a 17-pounder gun they could get off the production line for themselves. Another problem was a serious shortage of Shermans at the time, due to high combat losses. Even if the British would have offered to convert some of the Shermans, the US Army had none to spare.

It wasn't until December 1944 and early 1945 that the Army had extra Shermans that could be converted by the British to mount the 17-pounder gun. The British eventually converted 160 Shermans into Fireflies. More couldn't be built since the British couldn't supply enough ammunition to support them in the field. It is unclear from Army records if any of these vehicles saw combat.

Chapter 8

The Korean War

In 1948 the division between North and South Korea was referred to the United Nations (UN). The UN sent a commission to supervise free elections throughout the country. The Soviet authorities, declaring the UN project illegal, refused the commission entry above the 38th Parallel. The UN sponsored an elected government in the southern half of the peninsula, which in August 1948 became the Republic of Korea. The Soviets countered by forming a puppet government above the 38th parallel, known as the Democratic People's Republic of Korea.

Shortly thereafter, both the Soviets and Americans withdrew their occupation forces except for advisory personnel. The North Korean government promoted and supported an insurgency in South Korea. When this failed, the North Koreans attacked in force, sending their army across the 38th parallel on Sunday, June

Protected against Red Chinese counterbattery artillery fire, this M4A3 Sherman tank armed with a 76mm gun blasts away at Communist bunkers about 800yd away from its position on September 1, 1952. Notice the numerous empty shell casings from the 76mm main gun that have been pushed out of the vehicle's pistol port. *US Army*

25, 1950. The North Koreans quickly crushed the very lightly armed South Korean defenders and marched on Seoul the capital of South Korea. After capturing Seoul, they regrouped and crossed the Han River, pursuing the South Koreans' military forces southward toward the port city of Pusan.

President Harry Truman authorized Gen. Douglas MacArthur to supply the South Korean forces and to survey conditions on the peninsula and determine how best the United States could assist South Korea. Two days later, the president authorized MacArthur to use air and naval strength against North Korean targets below the 38th parallel. The next day, the president increased this authority to include North Korea and authorized the use of US troops to protect Pusan, Korea's major port at the southeastern tip of the peninsula. Meanwhile, MacArthur had surveyed the situation and recommended that a US regiment be committed in Seoul at once and that this force be built up to two divisions. Truman authorized MacArthur to use all forces available to him. The understrength 25th Infantry and 1st Cavalry Divisions were commissioned from their occupation duty in Japan.

These divisions went immediately into action in Korea, but they did not have their Shermans. Because of fears that the Sherman tank would tear up Japanese roads and would not be able to cross over the lightweight Japanese bridges, the Army units in Japan had only been equipped with the M24 light tank.

The M24 light tank, armed with a short-barrel lightweight 75mm gun with a low muzzle velocity first saw service with the US Army in Europe in late 1944. Designed as a scout tank to also be used as a mechanized infantry support vehicle, it was not supposed to be used in tank versus tank combat. Unfortunately, like the first-generation of Shermans, the M24 light tank was thrust into a role it was not designed for.

Initially, it was thought that the small numbers of M24 light tanks sent to Korea would not be a major drawback, since the country's rugged, mountainous terrain with its few level areas covered with marsh-like rice paddies was not considered suitable for their employment, or that of the enemy's tanks.

The North Koreans, however, employed tanks, and on July 5, 1950, the first Army unit from Japan, Task Force Smith, was overrun by 31 T34/85s.

The first Sherman tanks arrived in South Korea in July 1950 to replace the less-capable M24 light tanks. Most of the Shermans deployed to Korea were M4A3 models armed with a 76mm gun and HVSS. Pictured is such a vehicle of the 32nd Infantry Regiment, 7th Division in Seoul, Korea, on September 26, 1950. *US Army*

Besides using the 76mm gun armed M4A3 Shermans in Korea, both the Army and Marine Corps also employed the M4A3 Sherman armed with a 105mm howitzer. The Marine Corps dozer-equipped Sherman pictured here is armed with a 105mm howitzer and travels up the banks of the Han River after a pontoon barge transported it across the river. *US Marine Corps*

(When the North Korean Army invaded South Korea, it had an armored strength of 150 Soviet-built T34/85s.)

First entering production in 1940, the T34 was armed with a 76.2mm gun. By 1943, because of new, heavier armored German tanks like the Tiger I being fielded, the Soviets fitted their T34 tank with an 85mm gun based on one of their anti-aircraft weapons. In 1944 the Soviet tank factories built almost 11,000 of them. Powered by a reliable diesel engine, the vehicle's wide tracks gave it excellent mobility across all types of terrain. The North Koreans had been supplied mostly with late-war production T34 tanks by the Soviets.

The North Koreans continued to employ their tanks in the early days of the Korean War with devastating effect. The few M24 light tanks available were totally outgunned by the T34s. The 75mm gun on the M24 could not penetrate the frontal armor of the T34. In the first combat action between M24s and T34s, two M24s were destroyed with the loss of one T34 tank.

The US Army activated new tank units equipped mostly with M4A3 model Shermans. The Marine Corps and Army both used Sherman M4A3 tanks armed with 105mm howitzers. The Marines also used 50 M4A3 tanks each armed with a 105mm howitzer and a flame-thrower unit. This version of the Sherman received the designation POA-CWS-H5.

The first Shermans arrived in South Korea in July 1950 and were quickly rushed into the frontline positions. Besides the M4 series, the M26 Pershing and the newer M46 Patton tanks, both armed with 90mm guns were sent to Korea. The Sherman, however, was the most numerous tank to see service during the Korean War.

During the early battles of 1950, when the UN force counterattacked, M4A3s engaged T34s on a number of occasions. The guns on both respective vehicles could destroy the other; so it came down to who could shoot first. The 76mm gun on the Sherman, coupled with its better sights usually gave the Sherman the advantage.

On September 16, 1950, the 1st Marine Division and the US Army 7th Infantry Division, both supported by tanks (mostly M26 Pershings) landed on the west coast of Korea at Inchon, behind North Korean lines. These forces pushed

inland rapidly and retook Seoul. Concurrently, US military forces in the southernmost part of Korea launched an offensive. Led by 1st Lt. Bob Baker, tank elements of the 70th TB, the 1st Cavalry Division, drove north of the Korean town known as Osan.

The Inchon landings and the breakout from southern Korea promptly drove the North Korean Army back into their own country. The war had not ended yet; for as the UN troops advanced across North Korea they were attacked by over 500,000 Chinese Army troops.

The massive Chinese Army quickly threw the UN forces back into South Ko-

rea. It wasn't until the beginning of 1951 that US firepower, in the air and on the ground, began to push the Chinese and North Korean armies back out of South Korea. After a period of attacks and counterattacks, the Korean War soon turned into a World War I type stalemate in which both sides dug-in along the 38th Parallel. By the summer of 1951, bunkerbusting became the main activity for the Shermans. The Pershing and Patton tanks used basically the same Ford engine as the M4A3 Sherman, but were 15 tons heavier. The result was that they were severely underpowered and could not climb the steep Korean hills as well as the lighter Shermans.

A Marine Corps M4A3 Sherman tank equipped with a dozer blade pushes two burned-out North Korean T34/85 tanks off a road. The North Korean Army lost most of its armored strength to US airpower. When the Red Chinese Army entered the Korean conflict in late 1950, they had decided to leave their tanks behind in China so as to not restrict their mobility in the very mountainous Korean countryside.
US Marine Corps

This Marine Corps M4A3 Sherman tank in Korea has two barrels. The barrel on the right is a 105mm howitzer, the other is that of a flame-thrower gun. Sherman tanks so equipped were designated as the POA-CWS-H5. *US Marine Corps*

Shermans in Battle

The following narrative, provided by the library staff from the Office of the Chief of Military History, provides a feel for Sherman combat action in Korea.

"The attack started with Lieutenant Nordstrom's tank in the lead. Within 100yd of the road cut Nordstrom noticed enemy soldiers hurriedly climbing the hill on the left of the road. He ordered his machine gunner to open fire on them. At about the same time he spotted an enemy machine-gun crew moving its gun toward the pass, and took these men under fire

with the 76mm gun. The first shell struck the ground next to the enemy crew, and the burst blew away some foliage that was camouflaging an enemy tank dug in on the approach side of the pass on the right side of the road. As soon as the camouflage was disturbed the enemy tank fired one round. The tracer passed between Nordstrom's head and the open hatch cover. In these circumstances he did not take time to give fire orders; he just called for armor-piercing shells and the gunner fired, hitting the front of the enemy tank from a distance of less than 100yd. The gunner continued firing armor-piercing shells and the third round caused a great explosion. Ammunition and gasoline began to burn simultaneously. Black smoke drifted east and north across the high ground on the right side of the pass, effectively screening that area. Lieutenant Nordstrom ordered the

commander of the last tank in his platoon column (Sgt. William J. Morrison, Jr.) to fire into the smoke with both machine guns and cannon. At the same time other tank crews observed other North Koreans left of the pass and directed their guns against them.

"Lieutenant Nordstrom did not move on into the pass itself because by this time it seemed to him that the enemy would have at least one antitank gun zeroed in to fire there and could thus block the pass. He remained where he was—about 70yd from the pass with the other tanks lined up behind his. Fire on the enemy to the left of the road tore camouflage from a second enemy tank dug in on the left of the pass in a position similar to that of the tank already destroyed. Nordstrom's gunner, firing without orders, destroyed this tank with the second round. There was another violent explo-

Sherman tanks in Korea also suffered losses in combat. This M4A3 was knocked out west of Masan, Korea, on August 12, 1950. While the official signal corps caption doesn't tell how the vehicle was destroyed, it can be surmised that an enemy antitank mine destroyed one of the vehicle's tracks. Not having time to repair the vehicle, it was pushed off the road so other vehicles could continue on. *US Army*

This M4A3 Sherman is from the 65th Tank Company, 64th Tank Battalion of the US Army. It had become bogged down in mud after it slid off a Korean road. *US Army*

sion, which blew part of the enemy tank's turret fifty feet into the air.

"While this fire fight was going on at the head of the column, the Australian infantrymen were attacking along the ridges on each side of the road. There was considerable firing in both areas. Lieutenant Cook's tanks, on the left side of the road, had been able to follow the infantrymen onto the hill and provide close support.

"In the midst of the fighting at the head of the column, the guns in the two leading tanks jammed because of faulty rounds. At that time a shell came in toward Nordstrom's tank from the left front. Nordstrom instructed his platoon sergeant (Master Sgt. Jasper W. Lee) to fire in the general direction of the enemy gun until he and the tank behind him could clear their guns. This was done within a few minutes, and Nordstrom, having the best field of fire, started placing armor-piercing rounds at five-yard intervals along the top of the ridge to his left, firing on the only logical positions in that area, since he could see no enemy vehicles. Following the sixth round there was another flash and explosion that set fire to nearby bushes and trees.

"The next enemy fire came a few minutes later—another round from a self-propelled gun. It appeared to have come from the right-front. It cut across Lieutenant Nordstrom's tank between the .50cal machine gun and the radio antenna about a foot above the turret, and then hit one of the tanks in Lieutenant Cook's platoon, seriously injuring four men. Because of the smoke it was impossible to pinpoint the enemy, so Nordstrom commenced firing armor-piercing shells into the smoke, aiming along the top of the ridge on the right side of the road. He hoped that the enemy gunners would believe that their position had been detected, and move so that he could discover the movement. Another green tracer passed his tank, this time a little farther to the right. Nordstrom increased his own rate of fire and ordered three other tank

to the right side of the road. Again he failed to hit anything. For lack of a better target he then decided to put a few rounds through the smoke near the first enemy tank destroyed. He thought the two rounds might possibly have come from this tank even though the fire and explosions made this very improbable. The third round caused another explosion and gasoline fire. With this explosion most enemy action ended and only the sound of occasional small-arms fire remained.

"Shortly thereafter, both Australian units reported their objectives secured. Since it was now late in the afternoon, the British commander ordered the force to form a defensive position for the night. It was a U-shaped perimeter with a platoon of tanks and an infantry company along the ridgeline on each side of the road, and Lieutenant Nordstrom's tanks between them guarding the road.

"When the smoke cleared from the road cut there was one self-propelled gun that had not been there when the action commenced. It appeared that it has been left to guard the west end of the road cut and its crew, becoming impatient when no tanks came through the pass, had moved it up beside the burning tank on the right side of the road, using the smoke from this and the other burning tanks as a screen.

"At 2100 that night, enemy infantrymen launched an attack that appeared to be aimed at the destruction of the tanks. Lieutenant Nordstrom's 1st Platoon tanks, which were positioned near the road about a hundred yards east of the pass, were under attack for an hour with so many North Koreans scattered through the area that the tankers turned on the headlights in order to locate the enemy. The Americans used grenades and pistols as well as the tank's machine guns. Gradually the action stopped, and it was quiet for the rest of the night. When morning came there were 25 to 50 bodies around the 1st Platoon's tanks, some within a few feet of the vehicles."

By early 1953, the Korean War was dragging into its third winter. Truce talks had been an on-and-off activity since late 1951. Both sides dug-in on the ridges and hills of central Korea and constantly engaged in a series of small-scale unit actions to achieve some local tactical advantage over their opponents. The following narrative describes an activity in

By early 1951, during the UN counterattacks on Chinese Army positions, many US Army tanks were painted with fierce faces on the front of the vehicles. The belief held by some of the UN military command was that the typical Chinese soldier was superstitious of cats or dragons. They thought painting such figures on tanks would instill fear in the Chinese Army units. This M4A3 Sherman tank pictured is armed with a 76mm gun; the vehicle's entire crew poses for the photographer. *US Army*

crews to fire into the same area. There was no further response from the enemy gun and, to conserve ammunition which was then running low, Nordstrom soon stopped firing. It was suddenly quiet again except along the ridgelines paralleling the road where Australian infantrymen and the other two tank platoons were pressing their attack. No action was apparent to the direct front.

"At the rear of the column, Lieutenant Cook had gone to his damaged tank, climbed in and, sighting with a pencil along the bottom of the penetration, determined the approximate position of the enemy gun. He radioed this information to Nordstrom, who resumed firing with three tanks along the top of the ridge

which Co. C, 89th TB, participated, in early 1953.

"The enemy positions in front of Company C were set up as a series of strong points. Each was connected with the next by a maze of communication trenches and tunnels. The individual positions in the strong points were either bunkers, constructed of dirt and logs, or caves. These bunkers were well dug in and followed the general dictum governing Chinese field construction—dig deep, cover thickly, and camouflage expertly. Embrasures in the bunkers were exceptionally small, and also well camouflaged. The weapons emplacements of the Chinese were in tunnels or caves, where the weapon could be moved forward, fired, and immediately pulled back into the protection of the underground shelter.

"A direct hit on one of these positions usually damaged it to some extent, but Company C's practice was not to report a position destroyed unless a secondary explosion took place within the structure. Extensive damage was caused on these enemy positions, but daily the Chinese rebuilt the damaged positions. Much of the reconstruction took place during the night, but occasionally work continued through the day. Many casualties were inflicted on Chinese troops who were in the open rebuilding positions damaged by tank fire.

"The range of the enemy field works taken under fire varied anywhere from 800 yards forward of the MLR [main line of resistance] to upwards of 2,400 yards. The majority of enemy strong points in the area were about 2,000 yards to the front of the tank positions. In the vicinity of Positions 8 and 9 enemy emplacements were located comparatively close to the friendly MLR. Enemy-occupied Hill 400 was about 800 yards from these two positions. On Hill 400 the Chinese had built a 57-mm recoilless rifle emplacement, and on occasion this rifle fired at the tanks of Company C, sometimes as soon as the tanks moved into their firing positions. The Chinese 57-mm rifle crew would fire only one or two rounds and then immediately move back into a cave before a friendly tank could return the fire."

The Korean War dragged on into July 1953 before an armistice was signed ending the conflict. Tankers played a major role in the successes our forces enjoyed.

As Sherman tanks tended to be used as dug-in fire support weapons, there were attempts to provide additional protection for their very vulnerable suspension systems. In this picture, a 9th Infantry Regiment, 2nd US Army Infantry Division, Sherman has been driven into a sandbagged position prior to a firing mission. *US Army*

On display at Fort Hood, Texas, is this Korea War-era veteran M4A3 Sherman tank armed with a 76mm cannon. *Michael Green*

Chapter 9

Sherman Variants

The US and British armies modified the Shermans in varying degrees to perform a wide variety of different roles.

Besides those Sherman-based variants that made it into production, there were also a large number of experimental vehicles that never went into production. Because of space limitations, these experimental vehicles will not be covered.

Command-and-Control Shermans

For frontline armored unit commanders, who required more elaborate radio gear to keep in touch with rear-area commands, additional radios were installed in certain key vehicles. World War II radio gear was large and bulky compared to modern equipment. More radios meant less room in the vehicles. The Germans removed the main guns of some of their command-and-control tanks to make more room inside the vehicles for the ra-

This platoon of Marine Corps M4A3 Sherman tanks are all fitted with the deep-water fording kit. Consisting of two large thin sheet-metal funnels, one covers the tank engine air intakes, the other attaches to the tank's rear exhaust system. Properly waterproofed and equipped with these two large funnels, the Sherman tank could operate in water up to 6ft deep. *US Marine Corps*

dios. To prevent the vehicle from being singled out as an important target, dummy gun barrels were fitted to the vehicle's turret.

The British and Canadian armies also modified a number of their Shermans into mobile observation posts for controlling artillery fire. To make room for all the radio gear needed, the 75mm main gun was removed and a dummy barrel installed. For most Allied Shermans used in the command-and-control role, the main gun was retained but the amount of ammunition was cut back to make room in the vehicle for additional radio gear. Since more radios meant more antennas, it was fairly easy for enemy gunners to spot command-and-control vehicles. To prevent this from happening, many Sherman units mounted extra dummy antennas on their vehicles to confuse the enemy about which tank was the real command-and-control vehicle.

Mine-Clearing Shermans

Many experimental mechanical devices were fitted to Shermans to allow them to remove German mines or destroy them in place. All of them had definite limitations and some could be used only in certain situations. The two types of land mines most often encountered by

US tankers were antitank mines and antipersonnel mines.

The first mine-clearance device was the rotary flail. Developed by the British and used by the Americans, it consisted of a large cylindrical rotor with chains attached. When rotated, the chains beat the ground ahead of the vehicle carrying it in the hope of detonating any mines at a safe distance. The British constantly worked on the basic device throughout the war and fielded a number of improved versions.

The first British-developed flail device fitted to a Sherman was known as the Scorpion. The US Army used the device in Italy, but it was not problem free. The flail itself was powered by two auxiliary engines mounted in an armored box on the right side of the tank hull. When the British developed an improved flail device known as the Crab, which was powered by the tank's engine, the US Army dropped the Scorpion device and employed the Crab system. Unlike the Scorpion system, the Crab device could be raised clear of the ground by large hydraulic arms when not in use. To steer the vehicle when the flail was operating, the crew had both a gyroscopic and magnetic compass. At the rear hull of vehicles mounting the Crab system were lights

Developed by the British Army in World War II, the rotary flail consisted of a cylindrical rotor with chains attached. When rotated, the chains beat the ground ahead of the vehicle, detonating any mines in the vehicle's path. Pictured is an Israeli Army M4 Sherman tank using an improved flail device known as the Crab. *Israeli Army*

Pictured somewhere in France on October 11, 1944, is this American-developed mine exploder device known as the T1E3 exploder. The mine exploder device when fitted to the Sherman was nicknamed the Aunt Jemima.

The Aunt Jemima detonated mines by its heavy weight, but this heavy weight also caused severe mobility problems for Sherman tanks trying to push it around. *US Army*

and a system for dropping markers to guide following vehicles through a mine field.

The US-developed mine exploder device fitted to Shermans was known as the Aunt Jemima. The Aunt Jemima (T1E3 exploder) consisted of nothing more than two massive steel rollers pushed in front of a tank, with one roller ahead of each tank track. Each roller was divided into five discs. Each disc was about 4in thick and 8ft in diameter. The two large rollers were about 11ft high (the Sherman was 9ft high) and weighed in at about 4,600lb each. The weight of the entire assembly was about 59,000lb. The roller chains from the Sherman sprockets drove the loosely mounted discs; the spacers were arranged and grooved to allow the discs to move. The T1E3 worked well in tests, but in service use the device proved difficult to maneuver. The few US units who used the large rollers quickly lost interest in them.

The US Army also used the T5E3 mine evacuator. An evacuator is nothing more than a plowlike device that cleaves through a mine field, depositing the mines on each side of a furrow. Usefulness of the mine evacuator is limited in rocky terrain. One hundred T5E3s were built during the war.

The Sherman could also be fitted with a bulldozer blade. While it proved to be most useful in many engineering roles, the Sherman bulldozer blade (M1) was originally designed to be a mine-clearing vehicle. Sixteen Shermans mounting the M1 bulldozer blade were sent with the invasion fleet on D-day to land on Omaha beach, but only six made it to shore. The result was that the engineer soldiers who were supposed to remove German mine fields suffered a 40 percent casualty rate as they did by hand what should have been done by machines.

Amphibious Shermans

Prior to D-day, the British had adopted a tank flotation device invented by Hungarian-born engineer and inventor Nicholas Straussler. Straussler's invention consisted of a collapsible float screen and a propulsion system. After successful testing of the device fitted to a British Valentine tank, it was adopted into British service. In military service it was known as the Duplex Drive (DD). It was nicknamed the Donald Duck by some.

Because of the insistence of British Maj. Gen. P. C. S. Hobart, the DD system was redesigned for use on the Sherman.

When fitted on the Sherman, flotation was achieved by use of a large collapsible rubberized canvas folding screen mounted on a mild steel platform. The platform was welded around the waterproofed tank hull at the fender line.

In the water, the Sherman fitted with the DD system was driven by two propellers. The propellers were 26in in diameter and when not in use would be swung upward to obtain adequate ground clearance for the vehicle. In the water, the propellers rotated in opposite directions and could be turned either hydraulically or manually for steering. Top speed in the water was about 6mph. The tank had a freeboard ranging from 2.5–4ft, depending on the type of Sherman used.

Steering in the water for the DD-fitted tank was done by periscope extensions for the driver and tank commander to see over the flotation screen, or by the tank commander standing on a small platform welded to the right side of the Sherman turret and steering the tank manually with a detachable tiller. The driver of a DD-system-fitted Sherman used a directional gyroscope during the final approach to a beach.

To collapse the flotation screen on the Sherman, the steel struts which supported the screen were unlocked by a hydraulic system and the air was released from the inflated rubber pillars. The rubberized canvas assembly was folded into place by elastic bands attached by metal rings to the inside surface.

In late January 1944, Gen. Dwight Eisenhower was given a demonstration of the DD system as fitted to British tanks. Eisenhower was so impressed with the system that he insisted the US Army use DD tanks in the upcoming invasion of Europe. Because of his personal intervention, the DD system was built in the United States. Eventually, three US Army tank battalions, the 70th, 741st, and 743rd, were trained on DD Shermans before D-day. A number of British and Canadian tank units were also trained and outfitted with DD Shermans shortly before D-day.

While Eisenhower and the British Army were enthusiastic about the capabilities of the DD tanks, the British Navy considered the entire concept a waste of time. They felt that the DD tanks were too vulnerable to rough water conditions

Originally designed to be a mine-clearing device, the M1 bulldozer blade, when fitted to the Sherman tank, proved most valuable in many engineering roles. This particular

M4A3 Sherman tank with the old style suspension system slid off a road after losing its left track to a North Korean antitank mine on September 6, 1952. *US Army*

Fitted with a Duplex Drive (DD) system, this American Army Sherman tank completely erected its waterproof canvas flotation screen before entering the water. In the rear of the

tank are the two propellers that propelled the DD-equipped tank at about 6mph in the water. *US Army*

This former Marine Corps Sherman armed with a 105mm howitzer has survived to become part of a private collection today. Painted in a post-war scheme, this particular vehicle is based on an M4A3 Sherman chassis with the late-war HVSS system.
Michael Green

and enemy fire. As events turned out, the British Navy was correct in its view about the DD tanks.

On Omaha beach, two battalions of Sherman DD tanks were to be used.

Rough seas forced the landing of one DD tank battalion by landing craft. Of the other US tank battalion which launched most of its tanks into the water, only two out of 29 ever reached shore. The rest were swamped by waves as high as 7ft. Contributing to the high losses of the American DD tanks was the fact that they had been launched over 3.5mi from shore.

On Utah beach the weather conditions were less severe than on Omaha and the single US tank battalion using

DD Shermans managed to get to the beach 28 of its 32 tanks. At Utah beach, the DD tanks launched 2mi from the beach, which no doubt helped increase their chance of reaching shore.

Of the other three invasion beaches (Sword, Juno, and Gold), the poor weather conditions that plagued the American landings also hampered British and Canadian units equipped with DD Shermans.

On Juno beach, 29 DD Shermans of the Canadian 3rd Division were launched from 1–2mi out to sea. Eight were lost

Pictured during the Korean War, South Korean Army soldiers cover this M4E5 howitzer-equipped Sherman from the 17th Regiment, 7th Infantry. The barrel on this 105mm howitzer was both shorter and thicker than the 75mm gun found on most early World War II Sherman tanks. *US Army*

coming in. The British 3rd Division, supported by the 27th Armored Brigade, launched 34 DD Shermans on another part of Juno beach and lost only two when a ship traveling in front of them swamped them with its bow wake. Most other DD Sherman-equipped units intended to be launched on D-day were carried to the beaches by landing craft.

In the Pacific, the Army and the Ordnance Department decided to develop a system that would allow the tank to use its main gun as it swam to shore.

To achieve this aim, the T6 device was developed. The T6 consisted of a number of compartmented steel floats attached to the front, rear, and sides of the tank. The float compartments were filled with plastic foam covered with waterproof cellophane. Propulsion in the water was achieved by the motion of the tank's tracks which gave the Sherman's T6 device a top speed of 4mph. The tank was steered by twin rudders on the rear floats connected by control ropes to the turret.

While the T6 device was seaworthy when compared to the DD Shermans employed in Europe, the system's size was a serious disadvantage. Fully assembled, the T6 was 11ft wide and almost 48ft long. Shermans with the T6 device were used only once during the war during the invasion of Okinawa on April 1, 1945, and only in small numbers.

For most of World War II, the US Army and Marine Corps had to depend

on naval landing craft to deliver Shermans to invasion beaches or shores. Since Shermans were frequently required to ford a certain amount of water after disembarking from landing craft, a deepwater fording kit was developed. The kit consisted of two large funnels; one covered the engine's air intakes, the other covered the tank's rear exhaust system. Properly waterproofed and fitted with the fording kit, the Sherman could operate in water up to 6ft deep.

Howitzer-Armed Sherman

One of the original characteristics of the Sherman was that the removable front plate of the turret, constituting the gun mount, could be designed to accommodate any one of five combinations of guns. One of the suggested combinations was that of a 105mm howitzer with a .30cal machine gun. Work on this mount was started in early 1942, shortly after the standard Sherman with the 75mm gun and .30cal machine gun went into production.

In November 1942, two M4A4s were modified to permit installation of the mounts and were designated M4A4E1 Shermans tanks by Ordnance Committee action in December 1942. The mount itself was designated T70.

Necessary modifications included substitution of 105mm ammunition containers, installation of gyrostabilizer equipment designed for the 105mm howitzer mount, and minor changes in stowage.

One pilot vehicle was sent to Aberdeen Proving Ground and the other to the Armored Force Board. Tests at Aberdeen showed that the 105mm howitzer mounted in the Sherman turret proved to be awkward for the crew to load and fire. The turret was also badly unbalanced so that the power traverse system would not work properly if the vehicle was on any type of slope more than 30 percent. Because of the test program, a number of features were redesigned leading to a considerable saving of weight and space.

At Fort Knox in February 1943, these modifications were agreed upon at a conference attended by the Army and the Frankford Arsenal. Other decisions made at the conference included: using a partial turret basket with seats for the commander, gunner, and loader arranged to swing with the turret; omitting the power traverse and gyrostabilizer; not requiring a complete recoil guard for the howitzer; and redesigning the interior to stow the 105mm howitzer ammunition.

Two pilot models of the Sherman with a modified 105mm howitzer installation were manufactured and designated M4E5. The modified howitzer was designated as T8. The M4E5 was based on the M4A3 or M4 tanks built by Chrysler. Approximately 4,680 were built between February 1943 and the end of the war.

Sherman Assault Tank

The US Army had hoped that the M26 Pershing heavy tank would be available by late 1944, but as this would not be the case, it was decided to use the Sherman M4A3 tank in the assault role by increasing the vehicle's armor and modifying the tracks and powertrain.

Preliminary drawings were presented and an agreement was made to manufacture 254 such tanks. Ordnance Committee action in March 1944 designated the vehicle as the M4A3E2. The work was put through rapidly, and the tanks performed well in attacks on German lines late in 1944.

The M4A3E2 was distinguished from the standard M4A3 chiefly by its increased armor. A new final-drive casting,

interchangeable with that of the standard tank, was provided. The front nose of the casting was 5.5in thick, reducing to 4.5in on sloping surfaces. Rolled armor, 1.5in thick, was welded to the sloping front plate of the hull, making a total thickness of 4in. A new turret with 6in of armor was provided. The gun mount shield provided 7in of armor. Rolled armor, 1.5in thick, was welded to the upper side plates of the hull. No additional armor was added on the side plates below the upper hull level or on the rear.

The standard VVSS and track were used. Because of the vehicle's increased weight, of about 84,000lb, extended end connectors were used on the outside of the tracks to maintain the ground pressure at about 14.1psi. Normal ground pressure for most M4s ranged from 13.2psi to 14.4psi.

The M4A3E2 tank was originally intended to mount the 76mm gun. But it was decided that the 75mm gun was a better infantry support weapon, so it was installed in all 254 production models built. In Europe, some M4A3E2s were later retrofitted with the 76mm gun. The M4A3E2 also mounted the same secondary armament found on other Shermans which included two .30cal and one .50cal machine gun. A 2in smoke mortar M3 was fitted in the vehicle's turret and provisions were also made for interior stowage of five M3 .45cal submachine guns.

Water-protected ammunition stowage was provided for 106 rounds of 75mm ammunition. The headlights, siren, and turret pistol port usually found on Shermans were omitted.

Power was supplied by a Ford V–8 GAA tank engine. The final-drive gear ratio was changed to provide for maximum speed of 22mph. In use, the M4A3E2 tank was nicknamed the Jumbo. 1st Lt. Charles Boggess, commander of Co. C, 37th TB, used one named COBRA KING to lead the link-up between troops of the 4th AD and the 101st Airborne on December 26, 1944, during the Battle of the Bulge.

Sherman Rocket Launchers

The German Nebelwerfer 41 was a surface-to-surface free-flight rocket launcher with a range of almost 8,000yd that impressed the Allies. It consisted of a six-round launcher unit that could be mounted on the rear of a half-track or on

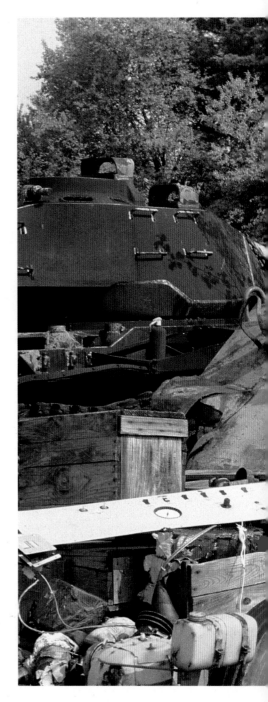

its own small two-wheeled towed mount. Firing its rockets in combination with other launcher units, it saturated an area of ground with HE rounds. While not completely deadly to tanks, it could cause extensive casualties to infantry, soft-skinned wheeled vehicles, and half-tracks.

The US response to the Nebelwerfer 41 was to develop a number of M4-mounted rocket-launcher systems. The first was the T34, which was fitted on top of the Sherman turret. The T34 used an

arm attached to the tank's main gun barrel for elevation and depression. Nicknamed the Calliope, the T34 weighed in at 1,840lb. The T34 consisted of 60 plastic tubes 90in long. The tubes were arranged 36 on top and 12 on each side of the elevation arms. The T34 fired the 4.5in HE artillery rocket. The entire T34 mount could be jettisoned if necessary.

A later model, the T34E1 launcher, had the elevation arm attached to the tank's gun shield. This allowed the tank

to fire its 75mm gun without jettisoning the launcher. Instead of plastic tubes, the T34E1 used magnesium tubes. The range of the 4.5in HE artillery rockets fired from either the T34 or T34E1 was about 4,200yd. In 1945 an improved version of the 4.5in rocket was produced. The stabilizing fins on the earlier rocket were replaced by canted nozzles in the base.

The Army continued to develop a number of improved tank-mounted rocket-launcher systems throughout the war.

This 105mm howitzer-armed Sherman rusts in a private collector's scrap yard. This version was known as the M4E5, and approximately 4,680 were built. M4E5s were built on M4 and M4A3 chassis.
Michael Green

But the only other US Army system using tank-mounted rockets to see action was the M17. The M17 mounted above the turret fired twenty 7.2in rockets off two rows of ten 90in rails. The M17 launcher was nicknamed the Whizbang. The 7.2in rocket weighed 61lb and had a range of only 230yd. A later model could go 1,200yd. The M17 saw combat in France and Italy.

The British Army also modified a few of their Shermans to fire 60lb aircraft rockets by mounting rails on either side of the turrets. Range was 400–800yd.

Sherman-Based Tank Destroyers

In 1941, the US Army created a new organization known as the Tank Destroyer Branch. By pooling most of its antitank weapons in battalion-sized units, attached to divisions, the Army believed that it would have a highly mobile antitank force that could respond to mass German tank attacks anywhere on the battlefield. The tank destroyer motto was "Seek, Strike, and Destroy."

The first production full-tracked tank destroyer was the M10. (Earlier tank destroyers had their gun carried either on light trucks or half tracks.) Mounted on the chassis of the M4A2, the M10 mounted an obsolete 3in naval gun in an open top turret. The M10 had a five-man crew and carried 54 rounds. Because it was fitted with lighter armor protection than the standard production Sherman tank, it could reach a top speed of 30mph. Production of the M10 started in September 1942 and ended in December 1943 with a total of 4,993 M10s built.

Ford Motor Co. was given a contract to build a similar vehicle, but on the chassis of the M4A3. The new vehicle, which carried the same 3in gun as mounted on the M10 was designated as the M10A1. A total of 1,413 M10A1s were built between October 1942 and November 1943.

The M10 first saw action in 1943, fighting against the Afrika Korps in Tunisia. The M10 served throughout the war from Europe to the Pacific.

The 3in gun on the M10 and M10A1 was not the perfect antitank gun as de-

Shown at the factory is this brand new M4A3E2 assault tank. Nicknamed Jumbo by the Army, it proved popular with tankers because of its heavier armor protection levels. Due to its extra weight, the basic Sherman chassis was badly overloaded and suspension and transmission breakdowns were common. *US Army*

Firing at night, this M4A1 Sherman tank is fitted with the T34 rocket launcher device. The T34 device fired a 4.5in HE artillery rocket. If needed, the entire T34 could be jettisoned. *US Army*

scribed by Earnest B. Forster who stated in a field report:

"While at Amperveiler I saw three dug-in Tank Destroyers with three-inch Naval open fire on two Mark Vs at a range of 800 yards, resulting in two ricochets on the German tanks and two tank destroyers knocked out, the third one withdrawing. The tank destroyer men held the element of surprise but Naval guns are not capable of knocking out the Mark V tank, unless at the proper angle."

A new 90mm antiaircraft gun just entering service with the US Army in 1942 seemed to offer better armor penetration ability than the 3in gun. Fitted into a newly designed turret in 1943, the 90mm gun was mounted on the hull of the M10A1 tank destroyer. In this new configuration, the 90mm gun armed tank destroyer became the M36 in July 1944.

The M36 carried 47 rounds of ammunition. Armor penetration was 6in at 1,000yd. When shooting at reinforced concrete, the 90mm round could penetrate 5ft at 1,000yd. When used as an artillery gun, the M36's 90mm gun could throw a round 19,000yd.

Between October and December 1944, 1,213 M10s and M10A1s were converted to M36 standards with the 90mm gun. At the same time, Fisher Arsenal built 187 tank destroyers by installing the M36's gun and turret on the unmodified hulls of M4A3 tanks. These unmodified Shermans with the 90mm gun were designated as the M36B1. Beginning in May 1945, a number of early diesel-powered M10s were converted to the M36 configuration and were known as the M36B2. Altogether, 2,324 M36s were built.

The British Army, which received almost 1,700 M10 tank destroyers, began replacing the existing 3in guns in 1944 with their own more powerful 17-pounder gun. In British service, the M10 tank destroyer with a 17-pounder gun fitted was known as the Achilles.

After the war, some of the very late-model M36s were supplied to other armies around the world. The most recent use of the M36 seems to have been in the fighting between the Serbs and the Muslims in Bosnia in the early 1990s, where ex-Yugoslavian M36s were used in this ongoing civil war.

Sherman Bridging Vehicles

To cross obstacles such as small

Because the 3in gun mounted in the M10 Tank Destroyer proved to be no match for thick, well-sloped German tank armor plate, in 1944 the American Army fitted a new turret with a 90mm gun on the M10 chassis.

Known as the M36, its new 90mm gun fired a larger, more powerful round than the 3in gun in the M10 or M10A1 Tank Destroyer. Pictured are M36s in Belgium on December 20, 1944. *US Army*

Using the chassis of a Sherman with its turret removed, the British developed a simple but crude bridging tank. Known as the Ark or Octopus, this vehicle drove into a stream or ditch that needed to be crossed. Once installed in place, the two hinged ramps were lowered allowing the following vehicles to drive over the now stuck bridging tank onto the other side of whatever needed to be crossed. *US Army*

This Sherman tank is fitted with a hull-mounted flame thrower that has replaced the .30cal machine gun normally fitted in the front hull of Shermans. The hull-mounted flame gun had an effective range of about 60ft. *US Army*

Canadian Sherman

In late 1942, the Canadian military was given the go ahead to have Canadian factories build the Sherman modified to fit their own requirements. This Canadian Sherman was supposed to replace the Ram II tank. The Canadian Sherman was known as the Grizzly I. It was almost identical to the US military M4A1. But much like the Ram II tank, US production of the Sherman was so large that there was no need to build them in Canada, and only 188 Grizzly I tanks were built. The Grizzly did not see combat in World War II. A small number were later converted into an antiaircraft tank by the addition of a new turret fitted with four fast-firing 20mm guns. It was designated as the 20mm quad AA tank and dubbed the Skink. Only one production Skink saw action in Europe during the war. It was used primarily against ground targets since the Luftwaffe had ceased to be a threat.

Flame-Thrower Shermans

Even before the attack on Pearl Harbor, the US military had started developing flame-thrower tanks. The first Shermans fitted with these units were six M4A2s used by the Marine Corps in July 1944 on Guam. Known as the E4-5 flame thrower, the device was fired from the hull-mounted .30cal machine gun position. Fuel tanks for the flame gun were mounted in the upper hull of the tank. An additional fuel tank could be fitted over the transmission. Another version of an auxiliary flame gun was designed to fit alongside the periscope in the assistant driver's hatch or in the turret roof. Both devices were limited by short range and low fuel capacity.

To overcome these problems, Shermans were fitted with a main-armament flame thrower. The Sherman's gun was removed and a flame-gun nozzle was fitted in its place. Under the turret of the new flame-thrower tank, known as the POA-CWS-H1, were four tanks carrying 290gal of fuel thickened with napalm. This fuel was propelled out of the flame gun nozzle by compressed air. Marine

streams or manmade ditches, the British Army developed and tested a small number of simple and crude bridging tanks, based on the Sherman hull.

They mounted a trackway that had two hinged ramps fitted at either end of it on the Sherman's turretless hull. These hinged ramps were supported by large metal posts which held up the ramps when in travel order. When time came to deploy the bridging unit, the driver drove the Sherman, carrying the device into the ditch or stream that needed to be crossed. The two ramps would be released and the following vehicles quickly drove to

the other side on the back of the now stuck Sherman. The vehicle was considered expendable in battle, but could be retrieved after the battle was over by other vehicles.

In World War II, the British Army took a number of worn-out Shermans with their turrets removed and converted them into fascine carriers. (A fascine is a tight bundle of brushwood that is used to fill ditches that are too deep for the tanks to drive across.) The converted vehicles were provided with a large open framed metal structure that carried the fascine. The US Army also experimented with a similar system in Italy in early 1945.

An M32 Sherman tank-based armored recovery vehicle of the 79th Heavy Tank Battalion of the 25th Infantry Division tows a disabled M24 light tank near Yechon, Korea, on July 19, 1950. *US Army*

Due to the short range and limited fuel of the hull-mounted flame throwers fitted in Sherman tanks, it was decided to develop a large flame gun that could be mounted in a Sherman tank turret in lieu of the 75mm main gun. Because the flame gun didn't look like a standard 75mm gun-equipped Sherman, it was decided to use salvaged 75mm gun tubes to hide the flame gun so as not to attract too much attention to the vehicle. Pictured on Okinawa on June 22, 1945, is an M4 flame-thrower tank firing at Japanese positions. *US Army*

Corps units used a number of these flame-thrower M4s to destroy dug-in Japanese defenders.

Because of Marine Corps wishes to retain the 75mm gun on their flame-thrower Shermans, a new design was constructed that mounted the flame-gun nozzle alongside the 75mm gun. This new flame-thrower arrangement was known as the POA-CWS-H5 device. Built too late to see action in World War II, the Marine Corps used them in the Korean War.

In Europe during World War II, the US Army was most impressed with a British flame-thrower mounted on their Churchill medium tank. While the flame-thrower device was fired from the bow machine gun position, like earlier Sherman systems, the difference was that the British system, referred to as the Crocodile, used a two-wheel trailer towed behind the tank that contained its fuel and pressurization system. Only six Crocodile systems were ever fitted to Shermans because of testing problems. Of the six Crocodile-mounted vehicles, only four saw service with the US Army in Europe. In action they proved popular, but the US Army never had more built because they believed that better US equipment would soon be available.

Sherman-Based Armored Personnel Carrier

The US and British armies made widespread use of lightly armored US-built half-track troop carriers. While the vehicles were cheap to make in large numbers, they suffered from limited cross-country mobility.

In August 1944, Canadian units fighting in France used a number of M7 105mm self-propelled howitzers and their British counterpart the Sexton chassis as the basis for full-tracked armored personnel carriers (APC). By removing the howitzer, a squad (ten soldiers) or more could be carried. Later, the British and Canadian armies converted a large number of surplus Canadian-built Ram tanks minus their turrets into APCs. In this version, the Ram tank was known as the Kangaroo. A number of war-weary British M4A2 tanks were converted in Italy to become APCs.

In 1944, realizing the need for mobile artillery guns that could keep up with fast-moving armored formations, the US Army began developing a 105mm howitzer based on a fully-tracked tank chassis. Initially selected were the surplus hulls of obsolete M3 medium tanks. Known as the M7, the British nicknamed it the Priest. Pictured is an early production M7 during a training exercise in the United States in 1943. *US Army*

Sherman-Based Self-Propelled Artillery

In late 1941, Maj. Gen. Jacob L. Devers, chief of the US Army Armored Forces (a former artilleryman), recommended that the Army take its standard towed 105mm field howitzer and mount it on the chassis of an M3 medium tank. He hoped to see produced a self-propelled artillery gun that could keep up with fast-moving armored formations.

After some tests at Aberdeen Proving Grounds and Fort Knox, the Army approved production. The vehicle was standardized in April 1942 as the M7. British soldiers in North Africa nicknamed the M7 the Priest because they thought the armored .50cal mount on the hull resembled a church pulpit.

The M7 was a simple vehicle with a 105mm field howitzer mounted in a box-like armored superstructure. The gun was serviced by a crew of five and could fire to a range of about 7mi.

A total of 3,490 M7s were built on the M3 chassis. The Pressed Steel Car Co. built a further 826 M7s (called M7B1) on the M4A3 chassis. Both vehicles were similar in appearance. The only real difference was the engines. Both the M7 and M7B1 remained in the Army inventory until after the Korean War. A number of them were later supplied to other countries as military aid.

It was decided in early 1944 to mount the Army's newest 155mm gun and its 8in howitzer on a second-generation Sherman chassis. This new tracked chassis had a wider hull than the typical M4-series tank, but it featured the newer HVSS system with 23in tracks. Unlike an M7 Priest, this new chassis had the engine moved forward behind the driver's position. The cannons were mounted on the rear of the vehicle in an open-topped superstructure. From February 1945 to May 1945, 418 of these vehicles were built. They were known as the T83. During the latter part of 1945, 24 of these vehicles were converted to carry 8in howitzers. In this configuration, it was known as the T89. In May 1945, the T83 was standardized as the M40. In November 1945, the T89 was standardized as the M43.

Production of the M40 with the 155mm howitzer and the M43 with the 8in howitzer was too late to see widespread combat action in the war. Only two early pilot models saw some action in early 1945. Both the M40 and M43 continued in Army service until the Korean War.

Sherman-Based Tank Recovery Vehicles

Before the war, the US Army had used large wheeled wrecker trucks (tow trucks) to recover disabled or stuck light tanks. As bigger and heavier tanks like the Sherman entered the inventory, the Army quickly found the best way to recover a damaged tank was by using another tank. By stripping the M3 medium tank of its guns and adding a winch and jib crane with an A-frame support mounted to it, the Army had produced its first crude tank recovery vehicle. As a shortage of M3 tanks developed, it was decided to use the chassis of various models of the Sherman tank as a new and improved

The M40 155mm self-propelled howitzer was developed too late to see action in World War II. Based on many Sherman tank components, the M40 saw heavy use during the Korean War. The M40 pictured fires its 155mm gun at enemy positions in Korea on June 30, 1951. *US Army*

Shown is the Canadian Ram I pilot tank. Built on the powertrain and running gun of the M3 medium tank, the Ram I and II featured a Canadian-built hull and turret.

The difference between the two models of the Ram tank was the main gun. The Ram I had a 40mm gun, the Ram II a 57mm gun. *US Army*

recovery vehicle. Since every model of the Sherman was used as a base for building a tank recovery vehicle, each model had a different designation. The M4 became the M32 tank recovery vehicle; the M4A1 the M32B1; the M4A2 the M32B2; the M4A3 the M32B3; and the M4A4 became the M32B4.

All of the M32s were equipped with a fixed turret made out of steel plates. Part of their standard recovery equipment was a 60,000lb-capacity winch and a movable crane-type boom with a lifting capacity of 30,000lb. Some Sherman-based armored recovery vehicles featured an 81mm mortar mounted on the front of the vehicle's hull. It was used to fire smoke shells to help hide the recovery of vehicles when under enemy fire.

As the Sherman was improved, so were the tank recovery vehicles of the M32 series. Later models featured the wider tracks of the HVSS system as well as all the other internal changes found in second-generation M4s.

By the Korean War, the US Army had developed a new tank recovery vehicle based on an M4A3 Sherman chassis. Known as the M74, this vehicle had a 90,000lb-capacity winch, a hydraulically operated boom and, unlike the earlier M32 series, a dozer blade at the front of the vehicle.

The British Army also had developed a number of different tank recovery vehicles based on the Sherman. The first version was nothing more than an M4 with its turret removed and replaced with a flat steel armor plate with a small hatch. A jib crane could be installed at the front of the vehicle known as the Sherman ARV I. Later versions had a fixed turret, mounting a dummy 75mm cannon, a jib crane and A-frame and spade assembly at the rear of the vehicle. It was known as the ARV II. When the British Army was supplied with the M32 series of armored recovery vehicles, they gave it the designation ARV III.

Preparing for D-day, the British Army converted a small number of ARV I chassis into BARVs. This was done by the installation of a tall superstructure. Completely waterproofed, the British BARV was used on the Normandy invasion beaches to rescue tanks and other vehicles that were stuck in the surf line. BARVs remained in postwar British military service for many years after the war.

Chapter 10

Shermans In Postwar Foreign Service

The British and Russian armies discarded their Shermans shortly after the war in favor of their own tanks, but the French Army continued to use them until the early 1950s when M47 Patton tanks replaced them.

The only combat use French Shermans saw after the war was in Indochina during the late 1940s. In 1946, the French Expeditionary Force, which included a number of M4A1s armed with 75mm guns, landed in what is now known as Vietnam. The force's job was to fight the Viet Minh. The French Shermans were replaced with new M24 light tanks by 1950.

After World War II, the French Army used a large number of American-built armored vehicles, including Sherman tanks, until they could rebuild their own tank-building industry. Pictured shortly before a parade on April 26, 1951, in Marburg, Germany, is a line of French Sherman tanks. The vehicle in the foreground is an M4A1 76mm gun-armed Sherman tank fitted with the late-war HVSS system. The Sherman tanks in the background consist of a combination of 105mm howitzer-equipped Shermans with the older VVSS system and additional M4A1 Shermans with 76mm guns. *US Army*

The vast number of leftover Shermans piled up in European scrap yards proved a fertile resource for rebuilding the Belgian tank force. The leftover Shermans were the mainstay of their army until the early 1950s.

Italy decided that the fastest way to build up its armored forces after the war was to buy from scrap dealers all the different types of M4s they could afford. These M4s were replaced in the early 1950s.

As the Cold War grew in intensity, US political and military leaders decided that they would even help rebuild the armies of Germany and Japan.

The Japanese Self-Defense Force was supplied with 76mm gun armed Shermans and Sherman-based armored recovery vehicles (ARVs). West Germany never used any Sherman tanks, but they did use a small number of M7 Priest self-propelled howitzers and Sherman-based ARVs. Both countries soon replaced these vehicles when the United States supplied newer post-war tanks.

The list of countries that have used or still use the Sherman or any of its variants is almost endless. From South America to Mexico, from the Philippines to South Korea and then on to Africa, with the small African country of Uganda being included, the Sherman has been almost everywhere at one time or another.

Of the many countries around the world that have used the Sherman over the decades since the war, only three have used them in large-scale combat encounters.

India and Pakistan, always wary of each other, found themselves in a border dispute in September 1965 that escalated into a month-long orgy of mutual destruction. Both armies were equipped primarily with US- and British-made arms, including large numbers of Shermans. Neither side displayed much skill in the handling of their tank fleets. The result was the mass destruction of large numbers of tanks. The short conflict ended with a stalemate.

The largest user of Shermans in combat since 1945 has been Israel. Involved in a number of major conflicts with its Arab neighbors since 1947, Israel has been in a constant race to field as many tanks as possible. Because of funding and political problems with the major arms-producing countries of Western Europe and the United States, Israel was forced in the 1947–1949 War of Independence to depend on war-surplus Shermans from scrap yards (roughly 50), many of which were without guns or fire control equip-

This one-of-a-kind Japanese Army prototype bridge-launching Sherman tank is being driven in a parade sometime in the early 1960s. The bridge-launching unit is mounted on an M4A3 Sherman hull with the HVSS system. *Chris Foss collection*

Pictured in the middle of a large training exercise is this Israeli Army M4A1 Sherman armed with a 76mm gun fitted with the standard US Army muzzle brake. The vehicle is riding on a late-war HVSS system. The Israelis called any unmodified Sherman tank in their inventory M1s. *Israeli Army*

ment. The Israelis were forced to begin a long line of modifications to their Shermans which continued until 1979 when they were finally retired from service.

During the 1947–1949 war, Shermans without the standard 75mm or 76mm cannons were fitted with an assortment of weapons including German 77mm field guns from World War I and a number of spare 3in guns out of the M10 tank destroyer. For a handful of Shermans with demilitarized 105mm howitzers still mounted, Israeli personnel adapted tight-fitting metal sleeves which covered the holes that had been drilled in the barrels.

The few Israeli tanks played only an insignificant role in 1947–1949. Knowing that their hard-fought victory was probably only a short interlude before the next conflict, Israel started to look for more tanks.

An arms-control agreement reached between France, Great Britain, and the United States in the mid-1950s helped to maintain an equal balance of forces in the Middle East. Israel was unable to acquire additional tanks until 1954, when France agreed to sell them a variety of vehicles and weapons including M4s. By 1956, Israel had bought 150 Shermans from France. Most of these Shermans were armed with 76mm guns.

The Israeli military designated these vehicles the M1 Shermans. Some were fitted with both the older VVSS system and others with the later HVSS system. They saw combat in the 1956 war between Israel and its Arab neighbors and performed well against the Soviet-supplied Arab tanks. Yet Israeli tankers realized that they needed to have a more powerful gun fitted to their M1 fleet to keep them a viable weapon system for the future.

In 1954 Israeli weapons experts traveled to France where they worked together with French technical experts to design a modified Sherman turret for mounting a French 75mm tank gun. This French gun was merely an improved copy of the powerful 75mm gun fitted to the Panther tank. After much work, the Israeli fielded a company of these 75mm Shermans in the 1956 war.

Most of these early upgunned Shermans were based on the M4A4 with a Continental radial air-cooled gasoline engine. The Israeli designation for this vehicle was the M50 Mark I (or Super Sherman). Later versions of this vehicle had

134

By 1956, Israel upgraded their Sherman tank fleet with the high-velocity 75mm gun from the French AMX13 light tank. This gun had a muzzle velocity of 3,200fps, compared to the American-made 76mm gun, which had a muzzle velocity of only 2,600fps. Mounted in a modified turret, the new upgunned Sherman tank was known as the M50 Mark I (Super Sherman). This particular Super Sherman is fitted with the older VVSS system. *Israeli Army*

the original engine replaced with a 460hp Cummins diesel engine. Also replaced was the older VVSS system with the late-war HVSS system for any vehicle not yet modified. In this configuration, the vehicle was designated as the M50 Mark II. Most of the M50 Mark IIs were built on 700 M4A3 Sherman hulls, which Israel had acquired from a number of different sources.

Prior to the War of Independence,

the Egyptian Army had only one company (16 tanks) of British-supplied Shermans. After the conflict, the British supplied the Egyptian Army with over 100 M4A2 Shermans armed with the 75mm gun.

The Egyptians, like the Israelis, considered their Shermans undergunned and went to France for help. The Egyptians decided to upgun some of their Shermans with the same basic 75mm French gun the Israelis had mounted in their M50 Super Sherman. The Egyptians chose to mount the entire two-man turret of the French Army AMX13 light tank on top of a Sherman hull. This awkward combination did not prove successful in Egyptian service and only a couple of dozen were so adapted. During the 1956 war, the Israelis captured 12 of these strange-looking Shermans, plus 40 M4A2 Shermans.

After the 1956 war with Israel, Egypt turned increasingly to the Soviet Union

for its armored vehicles. What Shermans remained in its inventory were passed out of frontline units, into reserve units.

While Israeli M50 Super Shermans could and did engage and destroy Soviet T34s, Israeli fears of the Arab armies receiving newer Soviet-built heavy tanks like the JS-3 Stalin armed with a 122mm gun and T54/55s with a 100mm gun prompted the Israelis to look again to the French tank gun designers for a bigger and better cannon that could destroy any tank the Arab armies might use in the future.

The French, working on building a better tank gun for their own army, had developed a 105mm long-barrel gun that fired a high-explosive antitank (HEAT) round. The Israelis saw a lot of potential in this gun. Working together with French technical experts, they managed to modify the gun by shortening the barrel, thereby lowering its muzzle velocity within an

The M50 Super Shermans were based on both cast- and welded-hull tanks. As time went on, the Israelis continued to upgrade their Super Shermans with an American-made 460hp Cummins diesel engine. All Super Shermans fitted with the older VVSS system were eventually upgraded with the HVSS system. In this configuration, the vehicle was now designated as the M50 Mark II Super Sherman. The M50 Mark II Super Sherman pictured belongs to a private collector. *Michael Green*

acceptable limit to fit it in a modified M50 Mark II turret.

With a new gun and a host of other improvements, this version of the old Sherman became the M51HV. Its nickname was the Isherman. The process of upgrading an older model Sherman into an M51HV was expensive, complicated, and time consuming. As a result, not all Israeli Shermans were upgraded into the M51HV standard.

The 105mm gun mounted in the M51HV turret fired a non-rotating hollow charge antitank round at a muzzle velocity of 2969fps—good enough to punch through 14in of steel armor. Because of the blast from the shortened 105mm gun, early on the Israeli military fitted a large muzzle brake to the end of the gun barrel. This item tends to be the most easily identified feature of the M51HV. Also fitted to the M51HV turret was a dual purpose white and infrared searchlight.

During Israel's 1967 Six Day War, the M51HV and M50 were used on all fronts; fighting the Egyptian, Syrian, and Jordanian armies. It was on the Israeli Central Front fighting the Jordanian Army that the M51HV and M50 Shermans suffered their highest loss rate. The Jordanian Army, trained by the British and equipped with US tanks, was considered the best of the Arab armies arrayed against Israel in that war.

On the second day of the war, Israeli Shermans crossed into Jordan in the darkness of the early morning hours. A Jordanian battalion of M47 Patton tanks armed with 90mm guns were hidden in the olive groves near the town of Jenin. When the Israeli tanks got close enough, the Jordanians let loose with a heavy barrage of fire that left a number of burning and destroyed Israeli Shermans. The Israelis quickly regrouped and counterattacked, but were beaten back by the defending Jordanian tanks.

Like most Israeli military equipment, this M50 Mark II Super Sherman was used for many years and saw combat on several occasions. Even though it has been expertly restored, some battle nicks are still apparent. *Michael Green*

The Israeli unit commander decided that a frontal attack was useless and instead ordered his tanks to fake a retreat, hoping that the Jordanian tanks would fall for his ruse and leave their defensive positions. The ruse worked and the Jordanian tanks now advanced into an Israeli ambush which effectively destroyed their battalion.

A few hours later, Jordanian M48 Patton tanks advancing on the now Israeli-occupied town of Jenin ran head-on into the Israeli Shermans coming out to meet them. Since the Jordanian Patton tanks saw the Israelis first, they deployed

into defensive positions and in the following battle they destroyed 17 Israeli Shermans. After regrouping, the Israeli Shermans counterattacked but suffered additional losses. Unable to defeat the Jordanian tank formations, the Israeli military ground units called on their air force to attack the Jordanians. It took until the next morning, after endless waves of Israelis air attacks, to destroy the Jordanian tank units.

On the northern border between Israel and Syria, the Syrians had for many years used the Golan Heights to shell Israeli settlements in the valleys below them. During the first few days of the 1967 war, Israel was preoccupied in dealing with the Egyptian and Jordanian military forces. However, by the fifth day of the war, Israel had removed the Egyptians and Jordanians as a military threat and now decided to deal Syria a military blow that they would not forget. In the evening hours of June 9, 1967, Israel

massed about 250 tanks (mostly Shermans) and about 20,000 soldiers for an attack on the heavily dug-in Syrian defensive positions on the Golan Heights. Leading the main attack were two companies of Israeli Shermans. The actual Israeli attack, which began on June 10, 1967, at 7:00am lasted until 6:30pm Saturday, June 11, when a UN-imposed cease-fire came into effect. When the Israeli tanks finally stopped, the Syrian military machine had disintegrated.

Israel's upgraded Shermans performed reasonably well against post-war Soviet and US tanks during the 1967 war. In the Israeli view, however, newer US and British tank offered more potential for improvement and most of their M50s were converted into non-combat vehicles. The M51HV Shermans were placed into reserve units.

On October 6, 1973—Yom Kippur—the combined might of the Egyptian and Syrian military forces were launched in a two-prong attack on Israel. While some advance warning was provided, in general the Israelis were not prepared for the strength or intensity of the Arab offensive.

In a series of bloody battles, Israel's military forces managed to blunt the attacks. Nineteen days after the attack, Israel had defeated the Arab armies. Due to the threat of superpower intervention by both the United States and the Soviet Union, Israel ceased its offensive operations and later withdrew from some of the Arab territory it had captured in combat.

By the 1973 Yom Kippur War, less than 250 of the roughly 2,000 tanks in the Israeli inventory were M51HVs, with a few older model Shermans still found in engineering units. At the time, the most numerous tank in Israel's service was the British Centurion armed with a 105mm gun.

As in the 1967 Six Day War, Israeli Shermans fought on all fronts against some of the best Soviet tanks of the day. Nevertheless, the Sherman was seeing its last combat use with the Israeli Army. In the early 1980s, Israel loaned a small number of their Shermans to one of the many Lebanese Christian militia units helping them defend their northern border area from terrorist attacks. Israel also sold Chile a small fleet of M51 Shermans.

Israeli Sherman Variants

Besides the Shermans modified in Israeli military shops, the Israeli Army over the years employed a number of Sherman-based variants including the Crab mine-clearing vehicle, bridge layers, M7 howitzers, bulldozer-blade vehicles, M4E5 howitzers, and M32 ARVs.

Armored Engineering Vehicles

To help clear obstacles from the battlefield, Israeli designers mounted the older American bulldozer blade and an Israeli-designed blade, which was fitted to a modified M50, minus its main gun.

The Israelis also developed on an M50 chassis a special-purpose armored engineer vehicle. Called the Trail Blazer, the vehicle features a large hydraulically operated crane, and two hydraulically operated dozer blades—front and rear—and a heavy-duty recovery winch.

Armored Ambulances

Israel has always been concerned with keeping its battle casualties to a minimum. To assist in getting wounded

To keep up with improved Soviet tanks supplied to the various Arab armies, Israel fielded the ultimate Sherman tank known as the M51HV (nicknamed the Isherman). Armed with a French-designed 105mm gun, the Isherman saw combat both in the 1967 Six Day War and the 1973 Yom Kippur War. The vehicle pictured has been converted from an M4A1 hull. The French-designed 105mm gun fitted into the M51HV Israeli Sherman tank had to be shortened to fit into a modified Sherman turret. To balance the long-barreled weapon, an extension was added to the rear of the turret as can be seen in this photo. *Israeli Army*

Pictured is the Israeli Army armored engineer vehicle based on the chassis of an M4A1 Super Sherman. Called the Trail Blazer, the vehicle features a large crane and dozer blades fitted to both the front and rear of the vehicle. Similar vehicles had already been developed and fielded by both Western and Soviet armies since the mid-1960s. *Chris Foss collection*

Pictured is a side view of an Israeli armored ambulance based on the chassis of an M50 series Super Sherman modified hull. As the Israeli Army later acquired large numbers of the new American-built M113 armored personnel carriers, older vehicles like the Sherman were withdrawn from service. *Chris Foss collection*

Mounted on the hull of a heavily modified M50 Super Sherman was the Finnish-designed, license built in Israel, 155mm howitzer mounted in a high-sided armored superstructure with overhead protection; the vehicle was known as the L33 in Israeli service. The L33 was designed primarily as a fast-moving counter-battery weapon. *Chris Foss collection*

A rear view of the unusual Sherman-based observation vehicle on display at the Israel Tank Museum. Seen is the observation platform, which could be raised by a large, scissors-type, hydraulically operated support arm. Also pictured are the two hydraulically operated support arms at the rear of the vehicle's hull. *Samuel Katz*

soldiers out of the combat zone as fast as possible, Israel built a number of heavily modified Shermans into armored ambulances in the late 1960s, using M4A3s with the VVSS systems. The engine was moved into the space formerly occupied by the turret basket. Where the engine used to be, the Israelis built a compartment large enough to hold a small number of wounded personnel. Exit and entrance was by a large split access door installed at the rear of the vehicle's hull. To provide additional overhead protection to the rear compartment, a large armored shield was welded over the rear hull area.

In between the 1967 Six Day War and the 1973 Yom Kippur War, Israel and Egypt engaged in a prolonged series of artillery duels and small-unit actions referred to as the War of Attrition. During this time, the Israelis developed a new armored ambulance. Using M50 hulls with the wide-track HVSS system, the Israelis moved the engine into the front, next to the driver's position. Instead of the cramped compartment found on the earlier Sherman ambulances, this new version was designed and built with an armor box located at the rear of the vehicle. The rear doors provided the exit and entrance.

When the Israelis received large numbers of American M113 APCs in the late 1980s, the second-generation Sherman ambulances was phased out of service.

Command-and-Control Vehicles

Normally, the Israeli Army used its large fleet of half-tracks as both personnel carriers and command-and-control vehicles. Unfortunately, the half-tracks had no overhead cover for its occupants. As a result, the Israeli Army used a small number of turretless Shermans in areas where artillery or small arms fire would prevent open-topped vehicles from traveling in safety. These vehicles could also be used to transport soldiers into areas under heavy fire.

The Israelis improved the concept by taking the M50 hull and moving the engine up front and building an armored compartment at the rear of the vehicle. Looking much like the ambulance variant, the new command-and-control Sherman entered service in 1967. The Israeli Army replaced them with newer vehicles during the mid-1980s.

One of the strangest looking Sherman tanks on display at the Israeli Army Tank Museum is this ex-Egyptian Sherman tank mounting an ex-French Army AMX13 light tank turret. This hybrid vehicle was not considered a successful design by the Egyptian Army and only a couple of dozen were so modified. Israeli military forces captured twelve of these vehicles during their 1956 war.
Samuel Katz

Self-Propelled Mortars

In the late 1960s, Israel modified a 160mm heavy mortar (built under license in Israel) to be fitted on the chassis of surplus M7 105mm self-propelled howitzers. The Israelis built an armored compartment to house the large mortar and its crew. To move the weapon up to its proper firing angle, a hydraulic system raises and lowers the entire mortar. The mortar itself weighs about 3,850lb and can fire HE or smoke rounds to 10,200yd. Carrying 56 mortar rounds, the eight-man crew can fire 5–8 rounds per minute. At least two machine guns can be mounted

on the superstructure. Used during the Yom Kippur War, the vehicle has now been phased out of Israeli service.

Self-Propelled Howitzers

The Israelis also acquired a fleet of M7 105mm self-propelled howitzers. But the newer, longer-ranged Soviet artillery used by Israel's enemies made the 105mm howitzer obsolete, so Israel turned to France for help. The French designers decided to mount their standard 155mm howitzer, the M50, on a modified Sherman chassis. The French moved the engine to the front of the vehicle and mounted the large howitzer on a limited-traverse mount in the rear. This combination provided mobile firepower, but the open-topped crew position and limited traverse of the gun were considered disadvantages by the Israeli military.

To correct these shortcomings, the Israelis designed their own 155mm M68 gun/howitzer. Mounted on an Israeli-modified M50 chassis, the new weapon was known as the L33. The L33 system had a fully enclosed, steel-armored compartment for its eight-man crew. Carrying

54 rounds, the L33 was designed from the beginning as a fast-moving counter-battery weapon to destroy enemy artillery units. The 155mm gun/howitzer on the L33 had a transverse of 60deg right or left and was first used during the 1973 Yom Kippur War. The L33 has been passed down to Israeli Army Reserve Units.

Observation Tank

One of the most novel variations on the Sherman chassis was an Israeli-developed observation tower. The Israelis mounted a scissors-type, hydraulically operated observation platform to the turretless hull of an M4A1 Sherman. The platform was steadied by two large hydraulically operated support arms at the rear of the vehicle. In civilian use, it is known as a cherry picker and can be seen mounted on some fire trucks in larger cities. Only three of these observation tanks were built, one of which has survived and is on display at the Israeli Army Tank Museum. Used during the War of Attrition to watch Egyptian military positions, these vehicles were phased out of service after the 1973 Yom Kippur War.

Selected Bibliography

Bailey, Charles M.: *Faint Praise, American Tanks and Tank Destroyers During World War II*, Hamden, Connecticut: Archon Books, 1983.

Barker, A. J.: *Japanese Army Handbook 1939-1945*, New York: Hippocrene Books, 1979.

Bradley, Omar N.: *A Soldier's Story*, New York: Popular Library, 1964.

Chamberlain, Peter, and Chris Ellis: *British and American Tanks of World War II*, London: Arco, 1969.

Culver, Bruce: *Sherman, in Action*, Carrollton, Texas: Squadron/Signal Publications, 1977.

Ellis, John: *Brute Force*, New York: Viking Penguin, 1991.

Forty, George: *M4 Sherman*, Poole, Dorset, Great Britain: Blandford Press, 1977.

————: *U. S. Tanks of World War II*, Poole, Dorset, Great Britain: Blandford Press, 1983.

Gardiner, Colonel Henry E.: *Tank Commander*, unpublished manuscript.

Hunnicutt, R. P.: *Sherman, A History of the American Medium Tank*, Belmont, California: Taurus Enterprises, 1978.

Icks, Robert J.: *Famous Tank Battles*, New York: Doubleday & Company, Inc., 1972.

Katz, Samuel M.: *Israeli Tank Battles*, London: Arms and Armour Press, 1988.

Ogorkiewicz, R. M.: *Armoured Forces*, London: Arco, 1970.

————: *Design and Development of Fighting Vehicles*, London: Macdonald, 1968.

————: *Technology of Tanks*, Coulsdon, Surrey, Great Britain: Jane's, 1991.

Sanders, John: *The Sherman Tank in British Service 1942-45*, London: Osprey Publishing, 1982.

Thompos, Harry C. and Lida Mayo: *The Ordnance Department: Procurement and Supply*: : The U. S. Army in World War II, Office of the Chief of Military History, Washington, D. C., 1960. (This volume is one of a multi-volume series titled the U. S. Army in World War II, which includes a large number of subseries covering all aspects of the conflict).

Zaloga, Steve J.: *The Sherman Tank in US and Allied Service*, London: Osprey Publishing, 1982.

Index